The Wind Still Whispers

To Jeff,
I hope you enjoy the book

Love
Gail P. Mah

Copyright © 2006 The Works of Gladys Oakley, Edited by Gail P. Main
All rights reserved.
ISBN: 1-4196-3388-0

To order additional copies, please contact us.
BookSurge, LLC
www.booksurge.com
1-866-308-6235
orders@booksurge.com

The Wind Still Whispers
Poems

The Works of Gladys Oakley, Edited by
Gail P. Main

2006

The Wind Still Whispers

TABLE OF CONTENTS

Introduction	xxiii
A Book of Verse	xxvii
Meet the Family	1
A Valentine	5
Love	6
My Mom	7
When Grandma Goes Upstairs	8
Aftermath	9
A Little Patience, Please	10
A Little Patience, Please	10
The Writing Housewife	11
Woman's Work	12
The Housewife's Serenade	12
Fate	13
Some Dreary Dawn	13
Returning	14
Had We Not Met	14
My Dad	15
The Men in My Life	16
Ode to a Man's Fishing Hat	17
Budget Babe	18
History Repeating	18
Man-Child	19
First Born	20
My Boy's Pockets	21
Curiosity	22
Woman's Touch	23
This Boy of Mine	23
To a Young Girl	24
Daughter of Mine	24
Gail	25
Gail's Mushrooms	26
Ginger	27
Karen with the Candid Eyes	28

Fun Poems 29
You Can't Win for Losing. 31
The Unbelievers 31
Statistic No. 116 31
Inhibitions Caused by Prenatal Influences 32
Subconscious Tendencies from Prenatal Influences 32
Inflation. 32
Arrows 32
Shaves there a Man 32
Bear in There. 33
It Pays to Advertize. 34
The Gremlin. 36
Plurality 37
Biceps C.O.D.. 37
Revised Edition 37
The Eyes Have It 38
Untitled 38
A Curious Matter 38
Zebra Question 39
The Morning After Hallowe'en. 39
The Giant 40
Hinges 40
Sisters Under the Skin 41
Death and the Lady. 41
Poems about Life. 43
Dad's Study 45
Credo 45
Three Sheets to the Wind. 46
Frustration. 46
The Saga of Old 31. 47
My Heritage. 48
The Harvest 49
The Harvest (another version) 49
Ballerina 50
Lucky Eve. 50
Pipe Dreams 51
Divided Me!. 51

The Choice	52
The Choice #2	53
Wonderment	53
That Compelling Urge	54
Beauty	54
The Little Things	55
Statistically Speaking	56
Dream House	57
To the Editor:	58
The Editor Regrets	58
Voices	59
Seventeen	60
Seventeen #2	61
The Search	62
Dawn	63
Be Limited	64
Conflict	64
Trees and I!	65
Trees and I	65
You Never Knew	66
Summer Storm	66
Strange Heritage	67
To a Conceited Male	68
Friend of Mine	68
My Hour With You	69
The Shepherdess	69
Wind-Song	70
Eulogy to a Dream	70
Dreams	71
My Dreams and I	71
Tempus Fudget	72
The Rebel	72
Qualifications	73
Reassurance	73
Don't Worry	73
Wisdom	74
You and I!	74

The Coronation	75
First shoes	75
The Wind	76
The Wind #2	76
Mother	77
Memory	77
Finis	78
Indian Raid!	78
A Dream for Sale	79
Anticipation	80
Reticence	80
House-Weary	81
Viewpoint	81
The Sands of Hope	82
The Sands of Hope (2)	82
Mine	83
The Perverse Female	83
I Needed You	84
A Disappointment	84
Temptation	85
Unplanned!	85
Lullaby to a Modern Baby	86
Spring	86
The World at Six A. M.	87
Comparison	87
Word Picture	88
The Elf in Me!	88
Whispering Wind	89
Nothing I Can Do	89
Enigma	90
Locked	91
Why?	91
Meet a Five Year Old	92
Problem Mother	92
Disqualified	92
Labelists	93
Until I know	93

Worth Living 94
When I Have Gone 94
The Vision 95
An Invitation 96
Dreaming 96
The Secret 97
Life 97
Near to Me 98
Only One Life 98
My Friends 99
In My Dream 99
Constancy 100
Dad and the Circus 100
Let Me Find Peace 101
Retrospection 101
To an Impatient Youth 102
Door-Mats 102
The Measure of a Man 103
Spring Magic 103
A Breath of Spring 103
Insomnia 104
Insomnia (#2) 104
The Duel 105
Whistle On! 105
The Inner Door 106
The Inner Door #2 107
Persuasion 107
Keyboard Notes 108
Clair de Lune 108
Is It? 109
My Mother 109
A Little Boy's Prayer 110
A Little Boy's Prayer (version 2) 111
Mother 112
One More Hill 113
The Puzzle 113
The Night 114

Rare Specimen	114
Apology for Dreams Unwanted	115
The Cynic	115
Extinction	116
Enigma	116
Enigma-Woman	116
Is There a Baby in the House?	117
Repentance	118
The Chronic Borrower	118
Repentance (2)	119
Perception	120
Here Lies Hope	120
Spectatorship	121
The Wisdom of a Fool	121
Inevitable	122
Symphony of Sorrow	122
Surrender	123
Supply and Demand	123
A Portrait of Mother	124
The Dreamers	125
Wishing	126
The Way of a Woman	126
Boundaries	127
Boundaries (#2)	127
A Poet's Prayer	128
Chatter-Box	128
The Point of View	129
Rendezvous	130
Introspection	130
Methodical Mind	131
Methodical Dreamer	131
To My Successor	131
A Single Mile	132
A Single Mile	132
Advice to a Fledgeling	133
The Cynic's Advice	133
Monochrome	133

Procrastination	134
Thanksgiving Night!	134
The Worry Wart	135
The Pessimist	135
Optimist	135
Pick-Up	136
Night Cry	136
My Secret Ambition	137
Resolution Time	137
The Giants Who Walk the Earth	138
Predestination	139
The Turning Point	139
Wanderlust	140
Spring	140
Advice	141
On Growing Old	141
The Two of Me	141
Lucky?	142
Regret	142
Shackled!	143
Rocking-Chair Judges	144
For Certain People	144
Point of View	145
Going to Church	145
The Reluctant Vision	145
Prayer Posture	146
Life	147
Little Talents (for bazaars)	148
One Woman's Thoughts on Bazaars	148
Prayer for a Crippled Child	149
Time Is a Thief	150
The Opinionated Male!	150
Haunted!	151
Foolish Pride	151
Prayer of a Selfish Child	152
Understanding Women	153
Problem No. 612	153

Lost or Strayed	154
Lost or Strayed #2	155
Delayed Action	155
As Long As There Are People	156
Once Is Enough	156
Almost Perfect	157
Friendship	158
Wondering	158
People I Can Do Without	159
Dislike	158
Poems about Love	161
Communicate, Please!	163
Untitled	163
The Hoarder	164
Freedom	164
Patterns	165
Fate vs. Love	165
If (with apologies to Kipling)	166
To the New Bride…	166
Plea	166
Love	167
These Things I Must Do	167
Our Love Has Changed	168
Your Name	168
Just For You	169
For You	169
Love Walked With Me	170
A Kiss	170
The Hapless Male	171
Autumn Song	171
One Life	172
Lost	173
Lost #2	174
Heart-Song	174
Awakening	175
Without Your Love	175
My Plea	176

The Time Has Come	176
Love Offering	177
For All These	177
Late-Night Thoughts!	178
Anniversary Thoughts	179
My Love	180
Choice	180
Lucky	181
A Silver Thread	181
To a Questioning Lover	182
When a Woman Loves a Man	182
Compensation	183
Untitled	183
Assurance	184
If	184
A Woman In Love	184
Spiritual Poems	185
The Star Who Ran Away	187
Epitaph for a Poor Rich Man	187
Epitaph	187
No title	188
Are We Really Thankful	189
As A Child	190
The Atheist	190
Trust	191
The Minister	191
I Saw the Hands	192
Four Things	192
Litany of Thanksgiving #3	193
The Christmas Spirit Comes to Our House	194
The Shadow of the Cross	195
Perspective	196
Alive	196
A Mother's Prayer	197
The Sick Child	197
Adoration	198
A Christmas Star	199

Title	Page
What Is It All?	199
Walls	200
There Is Never a Day So Dreary	200
Sudsy Thoughts	201
The Voice of God	201
The Least of These	202
Heaven	203
Heaven (2)	203
Mother Mary	204
The Master's Plan	205
The Master Plan	205
Untitled	205
Reflections	206
Untitled	206
Anonymous	207
POEMS ABOUT WORK	209
To the Lunchroom Girls!	211
Patience, Please	212
On the Lunch Line	212
On the Line	212
A Tribute to Nila	213
Kitchen Kapers	214
Lunchroom Ladies	219
Prose	221
Where Has Grandma Gone?	223
The Queer People (A Short Story)	224
Ban the Budget	228
A Christmas Tribute to Dad	230
A Prayer on Growing Older	232
I Must Go Shopping	233
A Housewife's Psalm	234
A Student's Psalm	234
What's in a Word	235
Ten Free Gifts for Christmas	236
Litany for Thanksgiving	238
Litany of Thanksgiving #2	239
An Easterner's letter to her son	240

Songs	241
Quit Messin' Around With My Man	243
For The Love Of Mike!	245
Who Stole Dat Leg?	246
Tears Run in My Ears	247
Michigan National Guard Anthem	248
I Tell My Heart	250
An Unfinished Poem	251

Acknowledgements

I want to acknowledge my family for encouraging me to continue with the book. I would especially like to thank my sister, Alice, for supplying the drawing used on the cover. I could not have completed the manuscript without the help of my nephew, David, who created the graphics and put up with his aunt's non-existent artistic skills, as well as assuming other tasks that allowed me to apply myself to entering the poems. I also would like to thank Denise Salo, who did the preliminary computer work that motivated me to continue and complete the book.

In memory of my parents who are responsible for everything that is good in me.

Introduction

The title of this book was, in a way, chosen by Mother. Her first book was <u>Whispering Wind</u>. Since this is a collection of her writings, the title, <u>The Wind Still Whispers,</u> decided itself. This is my chance to share the wonderful heritage our parents gave us. Mom wrote about many things, but mostly she wrote about every-day life. There are many poems about our Dad and poems about us kids. There are even poems about her work. Most of the poems reflect the light, loving environment created by these two wonderful people, Russell and Gladys Oakley. I have added comments about several of the pieces.

My mother always used a manual typewriter and carbon paper so she could send copies of her poems to people. I spent years going through everything I had in an attempt to collect my mother's writings in one place. Mother told me that if her poems were published, she wanted to pick the poems. She published one book in 1947. She told me that it was a lot of work. Traveling, and reading her poems at meetings was hard work and not as glamorous as I thought. She never did get that book put together.

She knew Edgar Guest quite well. In fact, he wrote an introduction to her book. She had many of her poems published. I have noted it where known. The poems with "Whispering Wind" beneath them were, of course, from her first book. The Dearborn Press used to call her Dearborn's own poet.

I began this effort in 1968. At that time, I was also using a manual typewriter. My typing skills leave much to be desired. I didn't get very far because I had to keep retyping the poems due to errors. In the 80s, I graduated to the computer. Although I went to work in the computer field in the 70s, I didn't own my own computer until the late 80s. My typing has not improved.

I have tried many things. I won an auction for 10 hours of computer work at church one day. I presented a stack of poems to be put on the computer and that became the beginning of another effort to get this done. When I got a scanner, I tried scanning the poems into the computer.

The scanner couldn't handle carbon copies on yellowed paper. Also, if you remember manual typewriters, you can get capital letters superscripted when you type fast. My mother typed fast and there was a lot of that in her poems. I have even tried voice recognition, but the software just can't understand the creative sentence structures of poetry. The only option was to type each poem myself. By the mid 90's, I was at a point where I had to check each poem I found to determine if I already had it on the computer because of the number of poems I had already transcribed.

It seems trite, but this is really a labor of love. Love for my mother and father. Love for my family. Last, but not least, love for the people who read this book or even one of the poems in it. I have been so blessed in the compiling. I just hope it also blesses those who read it.

I apologize for the categorizing of the poems. Many of them fit in more than one category, but I had to make a choice.

The very last poem, which seems fitting for the ending of the book, is an uncompleted poem I found. This poem is handwritten on a scrap of paper. I still have that scrap of paper as well as the originals of all the works in the book.

I encourage you to try your hand at completing this poem. I am interested in seeing all efforts in this respect.

Thank you for reading and feel free to contact me, especially with any endings or titles for the unfinished poem at the end of the book. You can write me at gailpmain@yahoo.com. Please use the subject "Unfinished poem", so I will be able to identify it immediately.

A Book of Verse

A book of verse should not be read
Like novels, page on page, instead
Glance thru the book until you find
The one that fits your mood, your mind.
Then take it to your heart and say,
"This is the verse for me today!"

Meet the Family

Mother was the youngest of three girls. Mom's oldest sister, Grace, played the piano and wrote the music to the songs found in this book. Mom's other sister, Alice, died when she was 18 from tuberculosis.

My father was the youngest of eight children. He was raised by his mother and stepfather.

My parents, Russell and Gladys Oakley married on August 16, 1934. They raised four children. It was almost like raising two families. I couldn't have chosen a better set of parents. My father was quiet, fair and understanding. My mother was an artist by nature. She would often say, "I can exaggerate. I have a license." Meaning, that is, poetic license.

The boys number two. Richard was born in 1935. Harry was born in 1937. Richard was named after King Richard the Lion Hearted and Harry was named after Mom's father, Harry Cox.

The girls also number two. Alice was born in 1945 and I was born in 1948. Mother tried for many years to have a daughter. She always wanted a girl and had the name all picked out. Alice was, of course, named after Mother's sister, Alice. I was named after Dad's favorite actress, Gail Russell. Mother always said she told the boys that if the baby was a boy, they could name him, and they chose Tom so we would have Tom, Dick and Harry.

My parents made no bold claims, but were respected and admired by all. My father was a plant foreman at a chemical plant. I can remember once how honored my dad felt because the union agreed with him in a grievance case. My mother taught Sunday School for over fifty years and tutored children for almost 20 years. My mom received a letter from one of the neighborhood boys she tutored telling her that he was in officers training and thanking her for making it possible.

Reading and education were of great importance to both my parents. The emphasis on reading and education is still prevalent in our family two generations later.

I don't want to bore you but this is an effort to honor my parents and I thought you should know a little about them and the family I love so much. My parents and my brother, Harry, have all passed on now. I just wish I would have completed this in time for Harry to enjoy it too.

My love goes out to all of my wonderful family. My love goes out to you too as you read.

Thank you

Gail

I found these two poems among Mother's things. They were written by her sister, Alice. I have added them here in memory of her.

A Valentine

What's sweeter than a sweetheart's kiss
On eve of Valentine?
What more could fill a heart with bliss
Than "Sweetheart, please be mine."?
What's keener than a girl and boy
Dressed up in lacy clothes,
Their hearts just thumping hard with joy,
And big red hearts in rows?
Around the bench on which they sit,
Four angels sweetly smile.
The boy says, "Sweetheart, you have it."
And she says, "You're worthwhile."
Oh why do modern maidens pine
For presents, row on row?
Why not be happy with a line
From the sweetest, bestest beau?

Love

The letter L means lots of things,
As Lohengrin and such,
And liquor filled with icy ale,
The tongue just loves to touch.
It also means some laughter bright,
That moves our hearts in joy.
And lilies of the valley, fair
So sweet demure and coy.
It might mean Luna, fairest moon
That sails the skies above.
But to my heart, the letter L,
Means just one sweet word, "Love."

Alice Cox 1/19/1930

This is the earliest poem I found. Mother wrote it when she was 12 years old. It dates to 1928/1929. This is about my mother's mother. Her maiden name was Anna Anastasia Jurkewiecz (pronounced yur-kev'-itch). We kids always called her Grandma Ann.

My Mom

Who is it dried my baby tears
And soothed my nighttime fears?
Who made me scrub behind my ears?
My mom!

Who taught me all the A B C's
My "Yes sir", "No sir", "If you please"?
Who sews the patches on my knees?
My mom!

Who comforts me when I am sad
And cheers with me when I am glad?
Who is it spanks me when I'm bad?
My mom!

Who always spots me when I try
To get away with just one lie?
Who makes the world's best apple pie?
My mom!

When I am sick, who makes me rest,
And rubs the camphor on my chest?
Who do you think I love the best?
My mom!

Grandma Ann used starch in all her wash. I can just imagine the clothes she washed standing up on their own.

When Grandma Goes Upstairs

When Grandma goes to Heaven,
All the little angels there
Will have their angel pinafores
All washed and starched with care.

Each halo will be polished bright
At just the proper slant.
Each wing with every feather curled..
They're ready for their chant.

And when they go to sleep at night,
Each Mary, Jack and Joe..
I'll bet their little angel robes
Are standing in a row.

Mother was born June 21, 1916. My mother's character is obvious in her poetry. It is hard to say one poem is about her and another isn't, but I have included here a few poems that are unquestionably about her.

Aftermath

If I should crash the Pearly Gate
I'd keep St. Peter in a state;
Tear my ectoplasm, scrape my knees
Climbing all the heavenly trees;
Wear my halo as a bonnet,
Even put a rose upon it;
I'd swing a mean and wicked lyre,
Play hooky from the angels' choir;
And usually have a torn gown
From clouds that I'd been sliding down;
Then some night when there'd be a fog,
I'd sneak in some stray, shaggy dog!
Though to be good, I'd always strive,
I'd be like when I was alive;
I'd spend my time, like Jack Horner
Standing in some cloudy corner!

(Whispering Wind)

There are two versions of this poem. Both have been published, so I have included both of them here.

A Little Patience, Please

When I grow old, I'll be sedate
And go to bed each night at eight…
But while I'm young, I'll have some fun…
At least until I'm ninety-one!

(Wall Street Journal)
Dearborn Press
New Yorker

A Little Patience, Please

When I grow old, as sure as fate,
I'll be a lady; poised, sedate
While I'm young, I'll have some fun,
At least until I'm ninety-one!

(Whispering Wind)

The Writing Housewife

The night is dark, the hero napping..
Blood is dripping from the sill.
From the door a gentle tapping..
A steady, firm persistent rapping..
It's the milkman with his bill!

Will the hero come, returning
Just in time to save poor Girt?
Higher now the water's churning,
Hear that sound.. the house is burning,
Oh my gosh, it's hubby's shirt!

A body's swinging from the rafter..
Was he stabbed or was he shot?
Hear the low, blood-stirring laughter…?
This will have to wait for after..
I've got chicken in the pot!

(Writer's Magazine)

Woman's Work
Or
The Housewife's Serenade

My day starts with the sun,
I'm many people in one.
I'm counselor, teacher and clerk,
I'm seamstress and farmer;
But still the gay charmer
For I mustn't look like I work!

I'm cook and I'm baker,
The raggy-doll maker.
I'm banker and barber and cop.
I'm dispenser of pills,
Consultant for chills,
And when I'm not busy... I shop!

When my long day is done
And I've tucked in each son
And my baby lies curled in a heap,
Then my time now is free...
It belongs just to me...
BUT ALL I CAN THINK OF IS SLEEP!

Dearborn Press

Sons are Richard and Harry
Baby is Alice

Father was born November 22, 1913. Although many of her poems were inspired by Dad, these were specifically about him. I am sure there are many more that belong in this section, but I have only included a few. One can easily identify more poems that are most likely inspired by him. This is especially true of the poems grouped under Love.

The first poem does a great job of summarizing Mom and Dad's characters. My dad was a wonderful, peaceful, quiet man. Compared to my dad, my mom was almost frenetic.

Fate

God gave you a peaceful heart,
Content by the firelight's gleam,
But He gave me the wind, the sun
And a poet's dream.

Some Dreary Dawn

If, waking on some dreary dawn,
You find your love for me had gone,
And you would go your way alone;
You would not hear me beg or moan.

Only my pillow, in the night,
Would know my loneliness and fright!

Written to Russ
(Poet's Herald)
(Whispering Wind)

Returning

"He's home!" Oh how that simple phrase
Erases all the endless days
When she was intimate with tears
And kept company with fears.

While children climbing on his knee,
Laugh and shout in ecstasy..
Her heart sings like a roundelay,
"He's home! He's home! He's home to stay!"

Had We Not Met

Had we not met would I have known
(We women wait for love to call);
The treasures that I tag my own,
A love by angels penned immortal.

How many things I might have missed
(And not the things men count at all);
Not just we met, nor that we kissed,
But woman-things men think are small;
To hear your footsteps on the walk,
To set your place, to pour your tea,
And then the long, unhurried talk,
The things that mean so much to me!

Had we not met. Oh, shun the thought!
(See darling, how my flesh grows cold)
To miss this love by heartbeats bought,
Nor walk together, growing old!

The following poem is written from the children's point of view, but it was definitely my mother's handiwork

My Dad

My dad's not a talking man
Like some I've met who quote
Long passages from books or know
Each wise thing Shakespeare wrote.

My dad's not a talking man.
Words seem to tie his tongue;
But when a thing needs doing..
You can bet that it gets done!

My dad's not a talking man.
In fact, words seem to bore him.
He goes quietly about his work
And lets his life speak for him.

Detroit News
(A tribute by Russ's children)

The Men in My Life

Now the men in my life
Have all varied in size,
Looks, in texture of hair
And in color of eyes...
Oh they taught me to live,
Love, laugh and depart...
Yet each holds a place
Of his own in my heart!

Yes, the men in my life
Set me up with the stars,
They bribed me with flowers
And sweet chocolate bars!
Each man said he loved me!
(Yes, they were the ones!)
So I lived with them all...
Father, husband and sons!

Dearborn Press
Beat of Wings (Oct. Nov, '48)

This is a fun, but true, little poem inspired by my dad and his favorite fishing hat.

Ode to a Man's Fishing Hat

The spatter and sprinkle of evening dew
Has given it sort of a green-blackish hue
While the lop-sided tilt of its now faded brim
Is worn up or down according to whim.

The puppy has tried all its efforts to tear it.
No self-respecting scare-crow would wear it;
Yet to him it's a symbol… a token… a friend!
Something to cherish and love till the end!

So tell him it's ugly. Say that it's spoiled.
Insist that it should be pounded and boiled
And soaked for thirty-six days in a vat,
But never discard a man's fishing hat!

The following four poems are definitely about my brother, Richard, who is the first-born child.

Budget Babe

Heaven bless thee, little man,
You're just what I had prayed for;
But how I could enjoy you more
If only you were paid for!

History Repeating

Now Algebra is Dick's concern
And I was much surprised to learn
That in the years I've been away
They still have found no shorter way
To learn if B can equal C
When A can do the work of three!

Dearborn Press

Man-Child

Dear Lord, Whom have You placed in my keeping,
That lies here beside me now sleeping,
The look of a wee angel still peeping,
Out of his little cherub face?
Will his music start people's hearts ringing,
Or the songs that he writes set them singing,
Or the sermons he gives keep on bringing
The Word to the whole human race?

Will he cures for diseases discover?
Will he help the wounded recover?
Will he crimes of the nation uncover?
Will he save the innocent time?
Will he help draft the laws of the nation,
Fight for right without procrastination,
Or paint pictures that cause great elation,
Or compose poetical rhyme?

These other things, Lord, don't really matter!
They are just a mother's fool patter.
For I don't want his life on a platter,
Or even a word or a sign!
To all men, let him be a good neighbor,
Let him not be afraid of hard labor,
And please, don't let him die by the saber;
This little man-child of mine!

(Whispering Wind)

First Born

One built a tower to the sky,
A symbol of his love.
One carved a figure from a stone,
A lovely pure-white dove.

One captured on a canvas back
The glory of the dawn.
One made a tomb of marble
With his slaves a living pawn

One wrote a song so beautiful
That angels, hearing, wept.
And one built a lofty castle
Where he, his treasure kept,

I have no slabs of marble grand,
No slaves to have things done;
But from my love more strong by far,
I offer you a son!

There is some debate as to whom, specifically, the poem <u>My Boy's Pockets</u> refers. I think it can easily be either one of my brothers. I always remember Mother telling me it was Harry.

My Boy's Pockets

Things I find in my boy's pocket:
One rabbit's foot, one light socket,
Two slugs and thirteen bottle tops,
A gun to use in playing cops,
Eight worms, (I think these all were dead),
And for melting one piece of lead,
A door-bell (this might be handy),
A very sticky piece of candy,
One lonesome and bewildered snail,
A letter he forgot to mail,
Two blown fuses, a length of rope,
And never used, one cake of soap!

Now, I don't know which could be worse;
A boy's pocket, a woman's purse.

(Christian Home)
(Whispering Wind)

Curiosity

For some girl I have yet to meet,
(My son is being quite discreet.)
He slicks his hair and shines his shoes
And wears Dad's ties by subtle ruse.

His shirt-tail by some sudden whim,
Now stays where it belongs on him
And lo, will wonders never cease,
His trousers keep a razor's crease!

What's baffled me for years, per chance
She changed with but a single glance..
What is she like, this rare delight,
Who transformed my son overnight.

Detroit News
Jack Birch Program

I remember my mother telling me the following two poems were about my brother, Harry.

Woman's Touch

A woman sure it must have been
Who picked the armored suits for men!
I think she picked that one design
Because she had a son like mine
Who thinks the parts below the knees
Just helpful aids for climbing trees!

Christian Home

This Boy of Mine

This boy of mine is boy all through!
There's nothing much that I can do
'Bout blackened eyes and bloody nose,
And dirt upon his Sunday clothes.

But then, I wonder: come the day
When he is heaven-bound to stay,
Will old St. Peter, at the gate,
Bellow, "Make that halo straight!"

(Whispering Wind)

The next two poems are about my sister, Alice. They paint a beautiful picture of a young girl.

To a Young Girl

Before she goes to sleep each night
Each thing that happens thru the day
Goes past her mind in full array.
She ties each one with ribbons bright
And tucks them tenderly away.

(Whispering Wind)

Daughter of Mine

You were but a name in my troubled mind;
A burning hope within my aching heart.
In other things, I could no solace find,
You were, of me, too much a part!

Gone are the days of dark uncertainty
And also nights in sleepless longing spent!
Oh, thank the Lord who let you come to me.
At last, I am content—content!

(Whispering Wind)

Mom's book was published before I was born. When I was a teen, I asked, "How come there are no poems about me?". This poem was the result.

Gail

I stormed Heaven's gates
With prayers, night and day.
Please send me a daughter
To brighten my day.

With the song of a bird,
A heart that is true,
One who looks like her Dad,
Yet has part of me, too.

Now how can I thank Him,
The good Lord above,
For one who came late
With a heart full of love!

The following is a poem about a science project I did in High School. I was to grow mushrooms, take spoor prints and compare the different types. It gives you an idea of my mother's keen sense of humor.

Gail's Mushrooms

She has brought books (a ton)
And she's read every one
On "Mushrooms.. the Fine Art of Raising."
Yet I wouldn't know a spore
If I met one! What's more
I couldn't care less when I'm braising!

She's wrestled with norms
And strange mushroom forms.
And her books all say they're nutritious.
But to this I will swear
With a steak (medium rare)
And potatoes (whipped) they're delicious.

Ginger was a toy terrier who was a part of our family for 17 1/2 years.

Ginger

I have a little puppy dog.
She stands about so high.
And wags her tail up to her ears
Each time that I walk by.

She has a coat of russet brown.
A vest of snowy white.
And snuggles close up to my feet
Throughout the long, long night

Karen is the first grandchild. I know this is about Karen, because her name is in the title and Mom signed it "lucky grandmother". I would know this is about my niece, Karen, even without those indications. Anyone who knows Karen would notice the resemblance. This leads to discussion of a problem I had when grouping poems. Mother never dated her poems (except the one when she was 12). One can tell a lot by knowing what was happening at the time the poem was written. My apologies to the family. I don't know whom many poems were about, but I do know Mother loved and enjoyed all her family. Many poems were inspired by them without getting their names attached to the poems. My mother and I talked a lot about her poems, but I didn't get them all gathered up until after she was gone.

Karen with the Candid Eyes

She looks at life with candid eyes…
Her innocence wears no disguise.
No artful looks, no cunning guile…
You see her eyes and then her smile!

With gentle heart she feels the need
To bring to flower a tiny seed,
And here and there a bunch of fur
Is happier because of her!

Now truth and beauty she can find
Where others are completely blind.
Who shares her laughter shares a prize…
She's Karen with the Candid Eyes!

Gladys Oakley (lucky grandmother)

Fun Poems

You Can't Win for Losing

I'm sure you must have noticed that
The foods you like will make you fat,
And things that you might like to do
Are immoral and illegal too!

The Unbelievers

There are people who would not even know
A dragon's three-pronged footprint in the snow.
Who never saw a gremlin hiding in the grass,
Or stepped aside to let a brownie pass!

Who crept up on a tulip in the early dawn
To watch a fairy Queen wake up and yawn..
Or looked out the window when the night was black,
Winked at the moon and had the moon wink back!

The nicest part of life has passed them by!
Aren't you glad we're different, you and I?

Statistic No. 116

People always seem to frown on
Patches put where they sit down on!

Inhibitions Caused by Prenatal Influences
Or
Subconscious Tendencies from Prenatal Influences

Did Eve
Believe
Adam
Had 'em?

Inflation

I burn the candle at both ends
And dance while others toil...
I burn the candle at both ends.
It's cheaper now than oil!

Arrows

I shot an arrow in the sky.
It hit a white cloud passing by.
The cloud fell dying to the shore.
I don't shoot arrows anymore!

Shaves there a Man

I wouldn't want to be a man
And shave for duty's sake...
I'd rather, as a woman, watch
The faces that he makes.

Bear in There

There's a Polar Bear
In our Frigidaire.
He likes it 'cause it's cold in there.
With his seat in the meat
And his face in the fish
And his big hairy paws
In the butter dish.
He's nibbling the noodles,
He's munching the rice,
He's slurping the soda,
He's licking the ice.
And he lets out a roar
If you open the door.
And it gives me a scare
To know he's in there.
That Polary Bear
In our Fridgitydaire.

It Pays to Advertize

The owl sits up in a tree
And hoots the whole night long.
The woodpecker does all the work
But doesn't have a song.

The owl sitting in the tree
We claim as very wise,
Which only goes to prove, my friends,
IT PAYS TO ADVERTIZE.

The Widow Jones lives all alone
And Farmer Brown did too
And though it seemed an awful shame
We didn't know what to do.

But Widow Jones sent him some tarts
And deep dish apple pies.
The wedding will be held next week..
IT PAYS TO ADVERTIZE.

Sweet Myra was a lovely girl,
But always out of reach,
And Tommy, smitten by her looks,
Would have no other peach.

Then Tommy got a plane and wrote
"I love you" in the skies
"My Tommy's smart," said she; 'He knows
IT PAYS TO ADVERTIZE!"

The Widow Smith had thirteen sons,
Each one a bashful lad.
"They'll never get a wife," she cried.
It made her very sad.

"There's oil on my land, I know."
She whispered soft and wise.
And thirteen brides moved in last week..
IT PAYS TO ADVERTIZE.

Poor Johnny never had a girl.
They wouldn't look his way.
No matter how he'd coax and beg,
No matter how he'd pray.

He bought a car, the flashy sort,
The envy of the guys.
And girls, he has them by the score..
IT PAYS TO ADVERTIZE.!"

The Gremlin

Oh, I wouldn't have a fairy,
Although they're light and airy,
For fairies are old-fashioned and passé;
But I have a little gremlin,
A bold, sassy little gremlin,
Who came to tea and never went away.

Now unless I'm quite mistaken,
He's the one who burns the bacon
And makes the toast as dark as cinder-block.
He's the one who blows the fuses,
And all sorts of things he loses
And he's the one who even stops the clock.

He puts sleeves into the butter.
He puts rust upon my putter
And plays piano when I want to sleep.
He pulls the tail of the kitten,
Likes to hide my other mitten,
And throws away the cards I want to keep.

He breaks up all my dishes.
He feeds chocolate to the fishes
And keeps me in a constant state of shock;
But though I didn't choose him...
I wouldn't want to lose him...
For he's the only gremlin on the block!

Plurality

We'll begin with a box and the plural is boxes,
But the plural of ox should be oxen not oxes.
We speak of a brother and also of brethren.
But though we say mother, we never say methren.
Then the masculine pronouns are he, his and him,
But imagine the feminine she, shis and shim.

So English, I fancy you all will agree,
Is the silliest language you ever did see.

Biceps C.O.D.

There was a young fellow named Rooney
Who by nature was really quite puny
'Til he answered an ad
For a new drug they had…
Now he's big and he's strong and he's looney!

Dearborn Press

Revised Edition

Mary bought a little dress.
The kind to please her mother…
The men didn't turn around and stare
And so she bought another!

Dearborn Press

The Eyes Have It

There was an old woman from Wheeling
Who said, "My poor eyes keep me reeling…
When I try to frown
My one eye looks down
And the other looks up at the ceiling.

Dearborn Press

Untitled

There was a young fellow named Hall
Who fell in the spring in the fall.
Would have been a sad thing
If he died in the spring.
But he didn't, he died in the fall.

A Curious Matter

There was a young lady named Rose
Who had four arms and twelve toes…
People shouted with glee
And said "Can't you see,"
"When she laughs, she wrinkles her nose?"

Dearborn Press

Zebra Question

I asked the zebra,
"Are you black with white stripes?
Or white with black stripes?"

And the zebra asked me,
"Are you good with bad habits?
Or are you bad with good habits?
Are you noisy with quiet times?
Or are you quiet with noisy times?
Are you happy with some sad days?
Or are you sad with some happy days?
Are you neat with some sloppy ways?
Or are you sloppy with some neat ways?"
And on and on and on and on and on he went.
I'll never ask a zebra about stripes again.

The Morning After Hallowe'en

The morning after Hallowe'en
My broom was not fit to be seen.
I said, "You look an awful sight!
I bet that you've been out all night.
No decent broom would go a-witchin'.
Now, go out and sweep the kitchen.
And when you're through, you comb your hair.
It's almost more than I can bear!"

(Whispering Wind)

The Giant

A giant came knocking at my door,
(He towered twenty feet or more)
To put it mildly, took me by surprise!
His hat was twice again as tall
And so I couldn't see it all.
His buttons were as large as apple pies!

"I was walking by the river
When I felt a sudden quiver,
And I knew that you had baked a lemon tart."
So he sat down at my table
And ate all that he was able
Which was all that I had made from the start!

He said, "This ought to make you glad.
These are the nicest tarts I've had
Since Noah's daughter made some on the Ark!"
He winked his eye and doffed his hat
Before I could say, "Skitter-scat!"
And promptly disappeared into the park!

Hinges

If we had hinges on our heads
There wouldn't be no sin,
'Cause we could take the bad stuff out
And leave the good stuff in.

Sisters Under the Skin

There's a bit of Eve in each of us.
But let me set you wise.
It's not an apple now we use,
It's deep-dish apple pies.

Death and the Lady

Death came to call on her,
An uninvited guest.
"I can't go now," she cried,
"I simply have to dress."

Death waited at her door,
A most impatient swain.
She braided up her hair
And took it down again.

Death sat upon the stoop,
A disillusioned man.
She tried another dress,
It didn't match her fan!

Death pounded on her door,
A most disgruntled gent.
"I'll come another time,"
Said he and off he went!

(Woman's Magazine)

Poems about Life

Dad's Study

Dad's study is the weirdest place
Piled high with patterns, bits of lace,
The hour-glass form of good Aunt Bess,
A dozen records, more or less,
The antique clock, a pewter mug,
A one-armed chair, a faded rug.

The room's so filled with things we've had
There's never any room for Dad!

(Mother's Home Life)
Dearborn Press
Detroit News

Credo

There's so much sorrow in the world,
So much of pain and fear..
Let not a word or act of mine
Provoke a single tear!

Three Sheets to the Wind

I'm bruised and battered.
I'm torn and tattered
And I look like the wages of sin!
But before you exclaim
Please let me explain.
I've been hanging the wash in the wind!

The Star (North Syracuse)

Frustration

Each dish has been dried
And hung in its place.
I've washed all the sweaters
And ironed the lace.

The baby's asleep
For an hour or more..
I've put out the cat
And bolted the door.

I've sharpened my pencils
And shut off the tank..
So what have I got?
My mind is a blank!

The Saga of Old 31

"There's trouble ahead," the engineer said.
"There's a curve that's high and steep.
We've old thirty-one to make this run
And our schedule we must keep.
She's been handled rough, but her boiler's tough
And she's always come on thru.
Can she make that curve without a swerve?
It seems we've much to do".
Her headlight gleamed and a young girl screamed,
"She'll surely jump the track".
But she gave a toot, a derisive hoot
As if to answer back.
We held our breath in the face of death.
We knew 'twould be the end.
But she put on steam with a wicked gleam
And slid around the bend!
The engineer wheezed as he brushed his knees
And said as he mopped his head,
"Just one hour more on the parlor floor,
Then, son, it's time for bed".

My Heritage

These things, (if I could leave behind,
A heritage so strange)
To you, I'd leave a searching mind
Not barred to healthy change.

To you, I'd leave a discontent
Of wrongs not made aright.
I'd leave one day in blindness spent
To show how great is sight.

I'd leave a night where hunger walks,
Another with despair..
Your heart will hurt when hunger talks
And teach you how to share.

I'd leave behind a valiant heart,
A penetrating sight..
And having fought 'Till death does part'
I'd leave, to you, the fight!

The Harvest

Man and woman, can't you see
A harvest there must always be?

Down thru the years, men sow the seed..
The seeds of peace or hate and greed.
Clash the cymbals. Dim the sound
Of babies crying on the ground.
Drive the wedge of fear to start
Tearing man from man apart!

But when Man's greedy little claim
Sprouts into pain and fire and shame
He wails from his bended knee..
"Look what my God has done to me!"

The Harvest (another version)

Man and woman, can't you see
A harvest there must always be?

Down thru the years, men sow the seed..
The seeds of peace or hate and greed.

Yet someday when man's greedy claim
Sprouts into pain and fire and shame
He'll wail from his bended knee..
"Look what my God has done to me!"

Ballerina

Put dancing slippers on my toes,
The gown I liked the best
And in my hair a red, red rose
When I am laid to rest,

For when a storm is at its height,
When fearful winds rush by..
When hearts are knotted up by fright
By lightning in the sky.

Then, look out thru the window pane
Perceive my silhouette..
For in the howling wind and rain..
I shall be dancing yet!

Detroit News

Lucky Eve

Consider Eve, the world's first maid..
All she had to do was raid
The nearest eucalyptus tree
For her new look; but not for me!

A scarlet blossom in her curls
Made Adam shower her with pearls
While I, with all my new attire
Can't even set one heart afire!

Woman's Day

Pipe Dreams

You settle down in your easy chair,
I snuggle at your feet.
You fill your pipe with Turkish blend,
So wild, yet strangely sweet.

Your pipe was carved in a Devil's mask
By an old one's skillful hands
And the smoke that rises in silent puffs
Has the scent of mystic lands.

The devil's mask jeers down at me..
He knows you soon will roam.
But now my weary heart is full.
My man has come back home!

Divided Me!

A part of me goes out with you
Each time you go away.
The other part stays home and does
The things it should each day.
It washes, cooks and cleans and mends
And wonders when the long day ends,
Will you return and love me. Then
I will be one again!

The Choice

A placid, squat house sits quietly by
'Neath the elm at the top of the hill.
The long winter's winds have weathered her stone
And in summer, moss clings to her sill.

Her windows wink gaily at all who pass by
And her heart almost bursts at the seams
With the shouts of the children, a dozen or more,
And their hopes, their faith and their dreams!

While, all slick and shiny, the road rushes on
Like Satan pursued by a bat.
Not stopping to nod or whistle a "Hi!"
He couldn't be bothered with that.

The rollicking road rushes on thru the night
Intent on his gay selfish quest.
Each thinks the other is foolish, no doubt..
Yet each does the thing he likes best!

The Choice #2

A placid, squat house sits quietly by
'Neath the elm at the top of the hill.
The long winter's winds have weathered her stone
And in summer, moss clings to her sill.

The placid, squat house sits quietly by
Content with her fire and cat,
While all slim and shiny, the road rushes on
Like Satan pursued by a bat.

The rollicking road rushes on thru the night
Intent on his gay adventuresome quest.
Each thinks the other is foolish, no doubt..
Yet each does the thing he likes best!

Wonderment

Years cannot dim the glow
Nor does the wonder fade
As on a busy street we meet
By prearrangement made.

My heart held high with pride,
Shines for the world to see
As in this crowded place
You smile and walk to me!

That Compelling Urge

Here I sit in darning splendor,
I, the family's docile mender!

How could they know who cannot see
The growing urge inside of me
To take these socks, add too, the broom
And build a fire right in the room,
Throw in that lamp, (forget the shade)
That afghan dear Aunt Gussie made;
Toss on my shoes, (I'm tired of brown)
Tear Uncle Sage's picture down,
Then Dance around in wild gyrations.
And shock the coming generations.

Yet here I sit in darning splendor,
I, the family's docile mender!

Beauty

She picked a pebble from the sand
And held it in her little hand.
Here was loveliness untold..
Blues and greens, deep reds and gold!

She heard their laughter, old and wise
And saw her treasure thru their eyes!
The lovely pebble from the sand
Lay cold and ugly in her hand!

(Detroit News and
Anthology)

The Little Things

It's not the big things one remembers
When he's far away from home;
It's his mother's queer old teapot
With the temple-painted dome.

It's the spicy smells of canning
That permeates the hall
And a bounding, wagging bunch of fur
That answers to his call.

It's the stiff, straight-legged soldiers
That march across his bed
And the peaceful quiet at the table
When evening prayers are said.

It's the jar of raisin cookies
Always filled up to the brim
Where a boy could fill his pockets
When he headed for a swim.

It's his Dad's contented manner
With his paper and his pipe
And the rusty tangy flavor
Of the apples when they're ripe.

It's not the big things one remembers
When his duty makes him roam..
It's the thousand, tiny little things
That made his house a home!

(Salvation Army Magazine)

Statistically Speaking

The man that I marry will have to be gay,
Considerate gentle and kind;
Be able to eat all the foods that I cook
And still keep a sensitive mind.

He'll have to know botany, music and art,
Romantically speaking, be tops..
He'll have to have money, a million or two
And let me charge at all the shops.

Now this kind of man does not even exist
But I feel there's a definite need..
So science, quit messing with serums and germs
And create this superlative breed!

(Wall St. Journal)

Dream House

I dream of a house upon a hill
Where everything is quiet and still..
Just the call of the whip-poor-will
Breaks the silence in the night!
There are gnarled oaks and stately pines,
Walls are covered with ivy-vines,
And thru the window, moonlight shines
On a baby tucked-in tight!

And when we say our evening grace;
Sunlight filtering thru the lace
Makes patterns on each well-scrubbed face.
Oh, that's a sight sublime!
But if I search and you're not there
My dream house crumbles in the air!
I want no dream that you don't share
Until the end of time!

(Whispering Wind)

To the Editor:

One fragile thought enclosed
For your inspection..
Please study carefully
Before rejection.

Note all its lovely lines,
Its vivid color..
See no clichés are used
To make it duller

The Editor Regrets

I rack my brain for adjectives,
For pronouns and for verbs.
To make my brain the keener,
I took to eating herbs.

My face is seamy, hollow-eyed
And then the doorbell rings..
But oh "The editor regrets"
Is all the mail-man brings.

All editors are monsters
With hearts of chilling ice
Who eat the flesh of authors
Served up with tea and rice!

Voices

Oh there are lights and laughter
And the motions to and fro
Of people as they enter
And people as they go.

And there are many voices,
Some are brassy, loud..
Some as soft as rain drops..
The voices of the crowd.

There is one voice I'm seeking..
I listen, but in vain.
Go, take your many voices
And leave me with my pain!

(Detroit News)

Seventeen

At seventeen, the golden age,
As Shakespeare said, "The world's a stage"
And you are waiting in the wings
With all the glow excitement brings
To hear the final cue!

You're seventeen! No one could doubt..
With dauntless courage looking out
Just waiting now your wings to try
And aiming right up to the sky!
Your fledgling days are thru!

Hold fast your dreams.. don't let them fade!
Don't lose the promises you made!
We need your wisdom, straight and keen
To right the wrongs we haven't seen..
Oh, how the world needs you!

Seventeen #2

At seventeen, the golden age,
As Shakespeare said, "The world's a stage,"
And you are waiting in the wings,
With all the glow excitement brings,
To hear that final cue!

You're seventeen! No one could doubt;
With dauntless courage looking out
Just waiting now your wings to try
And aiming right up to the sky!
Your fledgling days are through!

Hold fast your dreams; don't let them fade.
The world needs all your youthful aid;
It needs your vision, straight and keen!
Youth personified, seventeen!
Oh, how I envy you!

(Whispering Wind)

The Search

There is a longing in my heart
Like nothing I have known
For in a crowd I stand apart
From others and alone.

There is a hunger in its beat
That rouses me at night
And bids me search each lonely street
Until the dawn is bright.

My soul, it's longing magnified!
Is wise enough to see
The one for whom I searched and cried
Has now at last found me!

Dawn

Dawn slips into town
On soft, muffled cat-feet.
She trips thru the arches
And swirls down the street.

Like the wind thru the meadow
Her touch leaves no trace.
She's the essence of silence
Till she gets to my place.

Then she rattles the bottles
And pinches the cat.
With a loud, sassy blue jay
She stops for a chat.

She tosses the children
Right out of their bed
And starts ringing doorbells
Inside of my head.

With a cheerful loud cackle
She then wafts away
And leaves me to open
Another new day.

    Mother's note "How does dawn come to your house—like a bud silently opening its petals.

Be Limited

I can stand the burning sun,
Cold pestilence or blight..
But, deliver me, Oh Gracious One,
From a man who's always right!

Conflict

I wish there were two of me
So one could work and one be free.
Now duty's child would love to cook.
She'd thrill to suds and dust each nook.

She'd leave me free to heed the call.
A gaily dancing leaf in fall
A red-bird's flash against the sky
Or a turtle's solemn passing by!

How can I do each mundane task
And be a poet too, I ask?

Trees and I!

I'll marry you, my dear, but please
Don't take me where there are no trees!
Now life with you would be sublime
If there's a gnarled oak to climb
Or if a maple or a birch
Would tempt me with a lofty perch.

I love you, sir, but hope you see
That I must always have a tree!

Trees and I

I'll marry you, my dear, but please,
Don't take me where there are no trees!
Now life with you would be sublime
If there's a gnarled oak to climb
It matters not which house we buy
If there's an elm tree standing nigh.
To me there's nothing quite so grand
As some trees on a bit of land.
I love you, sir, but hope you see
That I must always have a tree!

(Whispering Wind)

You Never Knew

I loved you, but you never knew
How thrilled I was to walk with you.
Or how my heart would skip a beat
To hear your whistle on the street.
Then came that dark and dreary day
You said "Goodbye" and moved away
And never knew I loved you then...
When I was eight and you were ten!

Summer Storm

Come Darling, I will hold you tight!
Don't fear the lightning in the night;
God makes the flash as bright as day
To help an angel find his way!

The summer rains are angels' tears
For us and all our little fears,
And thunder is the rumbling sound
Made by brownies underground!

Strange Heritage

My grandma and my dear Aunt Pat
Just never got along.
My grandma's love was in her home,
Aunt Pat's was in a song.

My grandma loved the smell of soap,
(A mark of people good)
The sunlight through a window-pane,
The gleam of polished wood.

But Aunt Pat loved the smell of earth,
The twitter of the birds,
A moss-rose nestled 'neath a tree,
The poetry of words,

My grandma and my dear Aunt Pat
Have made a mess of me.
Since I take after both of them,
Just who is really me?

Mother's Home Life

To a Conceited Male

You think, I suppose, that since I met you
Other men have lost their appeal.
That I go dancing with them as a blind
So you won't know just how I feel.

That the phrases they use sound corny and dull
And sometimes not even quite bright.
You think, I suppose, that I wait for your call.
And DARN IT! I know that you're right!

Wall Street Journal

Friend of Mine

Life has its times of deepest stress
And days of greatest happiness.
It's then I feel our hands entwine.
I'm glad that you're a friend of mine!

I hope I'll never see the day
When you will cease to hear me say
"It's nice to know you're feeling fine,
I'm glad that you're a friend of mine!"

(Whispering Wind)

My Hour With You

When the moon above me is creeping
Thru a meadow of star-sprinkled blue...
When the world around me is sleeping
And I should be sleeping too...

Then I rise each night from my pillow,
A slave to her beckoning gleam.
We meet in the park by the willow...
A maid, a man, and a dream!

The Shepherdess

My flock of thoughts go climbing into space
Attaining heights that I could never gain,
While I, a frightened shepherdess, remain
Afraid to leave my snug and sheltered place.

Wind-Song

The song of the wind is broken-hearted…
Of loves who met and then departed
Not to meet again.
He sings of loves who've been forsaken,
Of loves asleep who cannot waken.
Of loves that might have been!

I listen from my tear-stained pillow.
He's singing thru the weeping willow,
Thru the swaying pine.
The lonely wind and I are keeping
A secret in our hearts and weeping.
For his song is mine!

Eulogy to a Dream

I watch the jagged rocks beneath
Then weave a gay and festive wreath
For in the ghostly moonlight's gleam
Lie remnants of a shattered dream!

Dreams

Magic carpets of the silent night
Where things I want or wish I might
Become are mine; but not to last..
For dreams dissolve when night has passed!

My Dreams and I

My dreams have been on every sea.
They've heard the Frenchman sigh, "Cherie",
And sipped of China's bitter tea.

My dreams have traveled far and wide,
With handsome ladies for my guide,
And Cadillac's in which to ride.

It's not that I'm the greedy one,
But must my dreams have ALL the fun?

Tempus Fudget

I lost a week... How fast it went!
Yet every single hour was spent.

Each staked a claim upon my day.
Each tore a part of it away.
Mother, housewife, teacher too..
I responded to each cue.

My song unsung, my book unread..
All the thoughts I'd write, unsaid.
Look at me now, a rusty tool..
Just a narrow, stagnant pool!

The Rebel

My mind says, "Other men there are
Who would be kinder, yes, by far..
Who would shower me with kisses,
Beg to change my Miss to Mrs.
And leave me not beset by fears
To wallow in my sighs and tears."

Yet my rebel heart unlocks the gate,
Lights the lamp, settles back to wait...
FOR YOU!   For YOU!

Beat of Wings (Dec. Jan. '48-'49)

Qualifications

My man doesn't have to be charming,
Attractive, or quite debonair.
My Man doesn't have to be handsome,
Or dark, or even have hair!

My man doesn't have to have money
Or pass an intelligence test.
Just give me a man that is mine,
All mine, and I'll do the rest.

Wall St Journal

Reassurance
or
Don't Worry

Don't worry, kind lady, if your small girl
Should like to give truth and fancy a whirl
Till you don't know where one begins or ends;
Who every stray cat and lost dog befriends,
Has no dignity, is painfully shy,
For she might grow up to write verse like I!

(Whispering Wind)

Wisdom

I wish that I could always be
As wise as that old maple tree
And though my dreams in cloud abound
Still keep my feet firm on the ground!

You and I!

You are the oak. I'm a willow tree.
Thru lonely nights you comfort me.
And when the dawn is breaking fair,
Your leafy branches brush my hair.

You shelter me from summer's storm,
From winter's blast, you keep me warm
And in the shade your branches give,
I am contented, dear, to live!

The Coronation

My young son came up to the door,
Tracked mud across my kitchen floor,
And, catching me quite unaware,
He placed a wreath upon my hair!

He kissed me once along the nose
While brushing dirt against my clothes.
He crowned me Queen, this lovely day,
Then, with a shout, went on his way!

You can't tempt me with furs or wines—
I wear a crown of dandelions!

Mother's Home Life

First shoes

Two little brown shoes with one heel run over..
Why should I keep them, now he's a sea rover?

There's nothing so wistful as baby's first shoes
And the memory of tumble-down steps after you.

I guided his feet when he proudly wore these..
Lord, hear my prayer and guide him now, please!

The Wind

The wind is a jealous lover
Always seeking to discover
If I should betray my mind
By idle thoughts I leave behind.

He runs light fingers through my hair
Reminding me he's always there.
He even blows with force of gale
To show me he is strong...and male!

The Wind #2

The wind is a jealous lover
Always seeking to discover
If I should myself betray
By listening to what I say!

He runs light fingers thru my hair
Reminding me he's always there.
He even blows with force of gale
To show me he is strong...and male!

(Whispering Wind)

Mother

A tiny baby tucked in bed;
Her cool hands on fevered head;
An answer in the lonely dark;
A lovely walk across the park;
A listener to a tale of woe;
A bandage on a bleeding toe;
Nut-covered cakes and apple pies;
An understanding heart for sighs;
A tender glance; a loving touch—
Did one word ever mean so much!

Memory

My memory is like a cloth
Wove thru with gold and blue..
Where here and there a rent appears
Whole days have fallen thru!

Finis

I'll take my hat from the old hall-rack,
My coat from behind the door.
I'll take the key that belongs to me;
But I'll come back no more!

I'll say "Hello Mike." At the old turnpike
And "Hello Jane." at the lea..
A turn to the right in the silent night
Will see the end of me!

Detroit News

Indian Raid!

Indians with painted faces
Peek at me thru window-laces.
Past the dog, now soundly sleeping
On their hands and knees are creeping..
Past the water fountain dripping...
Never faltering, never slipping.
Indians from far-off places
Dark of skin with dirty faces
Stealthfully their way are making
Toward the cookies I am baking!

Detroit News

A Dream for Sale

I have a lovely dream for sale!
It's of no more use to me.
It's just the oft repeated tale;
She found a new and different male,
While I was gone to sea!

A lover's dream of wedded bliss,
And babies, two or three!
A dream about that welcome kiss,
And other things a man can miss,
When he has been to sea!

My poor heart is bruised and sore!
From now on, I'll stay free!
I'll look at other girls no more;
Unless that one in Singapore,
Is waiting there for me!

My mother's notation: Typical male reaction

(Whispering Wind)
Dearborn Press

Anticipation

A part of me runs out to meet
Everyone upon the street.
But, when I see it isn't you,
There's nothing left for me to do.
Just turn with dragging heart to wait
For your footsteps at the gate.

Reticence

Don't look under or peek thru
The wall that's hiding me from you.
Yours is the great, gigantic things
That only wealth and power brings,
While I, oh how your world would jeer
At Little things that I hold dear!
But, oh my darling, can't you see..
My little world is right for me!

Anthology

House-Weary

I want no walls around me now,
No cellar, floor or ceiling.
No cozy nook, no silent book
For me the way I'm feeling.

To hear, while on a wind-swept rock,
The deep sea's cauldrons brewing,
Where there's no chintz, no somber prints,
To interrupt my viewing.

Or lie supine upon a hill
And watch the clouds sashaying.
Or close my eyes and listen, wise
To what the wind is saying.

Dear house of mine, you're not to blame
For all my restless surging.
Give me one day, one day away,
And I'll return, no urging.

Viewpoint

I looked at life and found it dim,
Devoid of warmth, a prankish whim
Of gods who use men for a tool.
Life looked at me and called me "Fool".

Detroit News

The Sands of Hope

Man is just a powerful brute
Who thinks, I'm sure, it's pretty cute
To flex his muscles at the beach
For every girl his eye can reach.

He thinks the girls will all admire
His trim physique in beach attire.
I don't, I'm sure, but just the same
Does anybody know his name?

Detroit News

The Sands of Hope (2)

To me he's just a robust brute
Who seems to think it's pretty cute
To flex his muscles at the beach
For every girl his eye can reach.

He thinks the girls will all admire
His trim physique in beach attire.
I'm sure I don't, but just the same -
Does anybody know his name?

Mine

What good are my eyes, if I not see
My own child's eyes look up at me;
Or hands, if I may not entwine
Hands with a little child of mine;
Or lips, if I may not recite
Nursery rhymes to her at night;
Or ears, if I not hear the song
Of childish prattle all day long;
Or feet, if her feet will not be
Beside me through eternity!

(Whispering Wind)

The Perverse Female

When you were here I said,
"If you should ever leave,
Don't think I'll sit and grieve
And wish that I were dead.

I'll seek some newer place,
I'll tease some gayer eyes,
And soon I know woman-wise,
I'll quite forget your face!"

Then why am I so sad?
Why haunt our trysting place?
Why seek to find a trace,
A glimpse of love we had?

I Needed You

I needed you; the need was strong.
The days were dark; the nights were long!
Why weren't you here where you belong?
I needed YOU!

I needed you; you were not there!
My hands touched only empty air.
I know now you did not care!
I needed YOU!

I needed you; my need was great!
Don't come home now for it is too late!
Other hands have closed the gate!
I NEEDED you!

(Whispering Wind)

A Disappointment

They picked a chief. You weren't the one!
I know just how you feel!
But tears will temper you, my son,
Like heat will temper steel!

It's better now, to learn to take
Each small hurt, one by one;
And though it seems an awful ache,
You'll be a better man, my son!

Temptation

I must be a lady
And not be indiscreet;
Mustn't serenade the moon
Or climb each tree I meet;

Mustn't listen to the wind
That teases round my face,
Whispers tauntings in my ear
Just daring me to race;

Mustn't go out walking
In the early morning mist!
Mustn't do so many things..
So sorry, can't resist!

Detroit News
Dearborn Press

Unplanned!

When my sweet mother tucked me in,
Coaxed me to eat each vitamin,
Watched how I sat and how I walked,
Guarded closely how I talked.
Kept my dresses neatly pressed,
I wonder if she ever guessed
You'd give a whistle one fine day
And all her plans would melt away?

Lullaby to a Modern Baby

Heart of my heart, it's time for bed
So snuggle down your curly head
For angels who have guarded you
Now have other things to do.

You don't want them to pay a fine
To Angels' Union, Local Nine,
For working past an eight-hour day
Just because you want to play!

So close your eyes; then two by twos
The angels can kick off their shoes
And soak their feet in twilight dew,
Then go to sleep dear, just like you!

Mom's comment "Things have changed"
Woman's Day

Spring

Why does it happen thus, that I
Who have much more than gold can buy
Become a restless, searching thing
At the first breath of early spring?

The World at Six A. M.

Just couldn't sleep. I slid outdoors.
Tried not to make a sound.
The grass squashed underneath my feet;
The sun rose big and round.

The world looked clean and dripping wet
Strung out across the sky.
(The angels must have worked all night,
Then hung it out to dry.)

There seemed to be no one on earth
But me. I ruled this day.
I made the birds sing out and trees
Grow just a certain way.

Just then I heard my baby cry,
A normal waking sign,
So I gave back His world to God
And I returned to mine.

Comparison

If I must leave my friends behind
My poor heart would sorely grieve!
But life could be much worse, I find,
If I had no friends to leave!

(Whispering Wind)

Word Picture

I paint a picture with my words
For all the world to see,
So clear that you can hear the birds
And feel the soft, blue sea.

But if I paint a mountain stream,
Your image I can trace,
And in a roaring fire-light's gleam
I see your tender face.

In every picture, you are there
A Quiet integral part.
For ever since I've learned to care
Your picture's in my heart!

The Elf in Me!

There's part of me that won't grow up.
It's like a gay and frisky pup!
They say, "Quit acting like an elf.
You have children now yourself!
Quite the lady you should be,
And full of poise and dignity!"
I suppose they are really right;
But before they are out of sight
I've climbed the nearest swaying tree.
Again I am myself and free!

(Whispering Wind)

Whispering Wind

The wind is always whispering to me
To follow him and live a life that's free!
For beauty in strange places would we seek;
To watch a sunrise, from a mountain peak;
To hear the mellow chimes of Mission bells;
And drink the dew from hidden fairy wells;
To climb a hill at night and then look down
On the blurred outline of a sleeping town.
I'd find the pot of gold at rainbow's end
If I would join my own capricious friend!

I listen to the wind that beckons me,
Then go into the house and make the tea!

(Whispering Wind)

Nothing I Can Do

I could no more control the tossing sea,
Or whether it be cloudy or fair;
Or change the robin's breast to azure hue;
Or harness all the winds that blow so free;
Or tell the sky what shade of blue to wear;
Than I could stop myself from loving you!

(Whispering Wind)

Enigma

Sometimes I wish, with my two hands
I could tear out this force
That shows me dreams of other lands,
Then mocks me in my course;
Won't let me be content!
"Go on and up. You are not through!
What need have you of rest?
One more, one more and better too!
This one might stand the test."
And so my life is spent.

This driving, nagging urge insists,
"It's study that you need!"
And when its rasping voice persists
A hundred books I read,
And still a hundred more!
Maybe, some day, I'll thank this curse,
This inner, nagging voice,
When in the beauty of my verse
The world will all rejoice!
Then rest will be a bore.

(Whispering Wind)

Locked

They read my verse and never realize
That all these lovely thoughts, for fear of jeers,
Have remained hidden in my heart for years,
And whispered to the wind, the seas, the skies!

Still other dreams deep in my heart I hide!
These lips of mine could never form the phrase
That would expose them naked to your gaze,
Until in lovely verses they are tied!

(Whispering Wind)

Why?

I lie on a hill, looking at the sky
And watch pop-corn clouds go wandering by.
Then I ponder God's ways and wonder why
We are; the sky, the clouds, the hill and I!

And I can't help wondering with a sigh,
If ever again, before I must die,
We can meet like this, although I might try,
We four; the sky, the clouds, the hill, and I!

(Whispering Wind)

Meet a Five Year Old
Or
Problem Mother

Questions, questions... all the day...
What makes the birdies fly that way?
Why is up up? What makes grass green?
Why, when I wash, do I get clean?
Why is it that my eyes are blue?
And why have I got only two?

Questions, questions, all the day.
I think that I've been gypped.
If only I'd been born
Encyclopedia-equipped!

Disqualified

Let those who would be good, be good
And those who would, be bad!
My life's too filled with love to cry
For loves they might have had,

My lips too warm from your embrace
To say what should be done.
My heart too lost to give advice
To those who kiss and run!

Beat of Wings

Labelists

The world's afraid, a frightened thing,
Of specters in the night.
They're humming tuneless whiffs of song
To put the ghosts to flight.

They peer, when no one's watching,
Pressed by the things they claim.
It calms their fears to label things..
Each one must wear a name.

Yet some there are, like you and I,
Who seek a further end.
So if a label we must wear..
Let all men call us "FRIEND."

Until I know

Darling, don't try to shelter me from woe;
I'll never be content until I know!
Though heartbreak lay in wait around the bend
His pathway I must follow to the end!
But if my fingers I should chance to burn,
Then quickly to the nest I shall return
To weep upon your shoulders, if I may.
Then rested, consoled, try another day
Until I know!

(Whispering Wind)

Worth Living

If I can take one child under my wing;
Give him the joy being wanted can bring,
And through the house hear his light laughter ring;
My life has been worth the living!

If I can teach him the wrong from the right,
And to keep his goal steadily in sight,
To get on his knees to his God each night;
My life has been worth the living!

(Whispering Wind)

When I Have Gone

As life goes on, year after year,
Remember, please, but not with tear:
How much I loved an organ tune,
The rain at night, a silver moon,

The freshness of an early spring,
The purple violets you would bring,
Your fingers running through my hair.
You see, I've had more than my share!

(Whispering Wind)

The Vision

In a vision one day
I heard an angel say
"Now is the time of decision.
Just one sound you must choose,
All the rest you will lose;
And there can be no revision!"
So I listened to all,
To the large and the small
To the soft and the loud,
To the humble and proud;
Heard the wind through the trees,
The soft, whispering breeze;
Heard the beat of the drum
In a band as they come;
Heard the waves on the shore,
A loved one at the door;
Heard a plane in the night,
A bird sing, out of sight!
I was making my choice
When I heard a wee voice
Ring clear as a bell, undefiled!
If I lost all the rest,
I'll have one I love best:
The laughter of a little child!

(Whispering Wind)

An Invitation

Come, sit by the fire
And we will conspire
To spend an evening that's free!
We'll tell all our dreams,
While the firelight gleams
And even have cookies and tea!

Who cares if it snows,
Or if the wind blows,
So warm and comfy we will be!
Before winter ends
I hope all my friends
Will come, sit by the fire with me!

(Whispering Wind)

Dreaming

I tell myself, "Your time is not free;
And don't you try any scheming!"
But I pay no attention to me,
And go right on with my dreaming!

(Whispering Wind)

The Secret

My heart cries out for forest land!
Your trees tall and majestic stand,
With lofty banners, all unfurled
To guard against a prying world!
For years a silent watch you've stood,
A guard honor, carved in wood!

Is there a princess, stricken dumb,
Just waiting for her prince to come?
Time and time again I've tried
To find the secret that you hide.
Each time your branches tighter press
So all that I can do is guess!

(Whispering Wind)

Life

I run to see what life will bring!
It's always some exquisite thing;
A bird's clear song, a budding rose,
The feel of grass beneath my toes,
The scent of clover in the air,
The soft wind blowing through my hair.
Tonight a moon of gold will shine,
And all that life can hold is mine!

(Whispering Wind)

Near to Me

Although it had to be
And we are miles apart,
You are as near to me
As each beat of my heart!

So I fear not the night
Or the cold winter's storm;
For love makes it bright,
Like a cloak, keeps me warm!

(Whispering Wind)

Only One Life

Just one life is so short a time
To spend with you, my dear;
Go walking with your hand in mine
Through each succeeding year.

Now, I have been a happy wife
As one can plainly see;
But, if you had another life
Would you live it with me?

(Whispering Wind)

My Friends

My life is like a golden line
All set with jewels rare,
For each one is a friend of mine
I've learned to know and care!

Now, hoarding is a thing that's bad
But this much you should know;
I'll hoard every friend I've had
And never let him go!

(Whispering Wind)

In My Dream

I've had so many dreams come true
That sometimes I'm afraid to sleep.
If in a dream, you said, "We're through!"
My heart and I, alone would weep.

Then someday, if you'd be unkind,
My heart would slowly fill with pain
And the thought creep into my mind:
My dream is coming true again!

(Whispering Wind)

Constancy

I gave my heart, my life to you,
And said, "Your way would be my way."
My love was strong and, oh, so true,
But, darling, that was yesterday!

(Whispering Wind)

Dad and the Circus

It seems that I can hardly wait
To take you through the circus gate.
We'll see the bear and kangaroo,
And monkeys dressed in gold and blue.
We'll laugh together at the clown
Who rides a camel upside down;
And, while we watch the Big Parade,
We'll have popcorn and lemonade.
While puppets dance upon a string
Your little hand to mine will cling.
Together we'll have lots of fun
When you're a little older, son!

But now I must turn down the light,
For you were only born last night!

(Whispering Wind)

Let Me Find Peace

Let me find peace in little things;
The lilting tune a robin sings,
A setting sun, a star-filled sky,
The pop-corn clouds that wander by.

Let me find peace contentment brings
In a world possessed of little things!

Retrospection

Ever since I was a little girl. Oh maybe three or four,
I've loved the tales that old folks tell and always beg for more.
I'd bribe my weary Grandma with a nice, hot cup of tea,
Then settle down upon the floor, my head upon her knee.
She'd tell how Grandpa courted her while still a girl in school,
And how he stole a kiss one day beside the lily pool!
How half the people died the time that small-pox swept the town.
Someone dug a single grave, then wrapped and laid them down!
My mind's eye sees the gown she wore to marry in the fall,
My ears hear rustling taffeta in a candle-lighted hall!

I hope a grandma I will be, when I have grown old,
Whose children gather at her knee to have a story told!

To an Impatient Youth

Why do you run, little man? Why run?
Why race thru the night to find the sun?
Can't enjoy this lovely hill,
The soft bird's song, the daffodil?
No time to stop and drink your fill?
Why run, little man? Why run?

Why do you hurry all the time?
Why force yourself to make that climb?
Why don't you stop and rest a bit..
The tea is hot, the fire's lit..
Come join a friend and sing and sit.
Why run, little man? Why run?

Why always peek around the bends?
Can't wait to see what tomorrow sends,
Can't relax this mellow day,
Join the gang awhile and play.
Got to be up and on your way.
Why run, little man? Why run?

Door-Mats

Women have been door-mats
Since that first life-like clod..
They keep their men from going in
With muddy feet to God.

The Measure of a Man

The measure of a man's success
Is not the things he may possess!
It's not his car, all plush and chrome.
It's not his new, tri-level home.
His job secure and, even more,
His name in gold upon the door!

The measure of a man in part..
What he holds closest to his heart!
A faith that's strong, a living creed.
He reaches out to those in need.
This man, twice blest! How much he cares
And with his brothers gladly shares!

Success will wither on the vine
If measured by the dollar sign!

Spring Magic
Or
A Breath of Spring

Magic is passé, they say.
It's hardly worth the mention.
'Twas just a ruse like button shoes
To claim our fond attention.
Then yesterday Spring came to pay
A visit thru my transom.
I wouldn't dream to trade one gleam
For all a kingly ransom.

Insomnia

I lie awake and pray for sleep..
I count horses, goats and sheep!
Three o'clock! I brush my hair,
Drink warm milk, try sleeping bare!

As I pace, how much I wonder
If you share the spell I'm under.
And as dawn begins to break..
Did you share my stay-awake?

Or are you a caddish number
Who'd kiss a girl and DARN IT, slumber?

Insomnia (#2)

I lie awake and pray for sleep..
I count horses, goats and sheep!
Pigs and chickens run about,
Some with glasses, some without!

Three o'clock! I brush my hair,
Drink warm milk, try sleeping bare.
Hear the rooster's early call,
Count the roses on the wall

Wonder if the milk will keep-
Five o'clock... I fall asleep!

Detroit News?

The Duel

Each Spring it happens this same way:
When comes the first warm, glowing day,
A gypsy, latent in my heart,
Awakens, coaxing to depart
Down winding highways, ribbon white,
Thru woods where fairies dance at night;
But housewife that I am (and dope)
I grab the ladder, pail and soap!

Whistle On!

The part that is me..
That people can see..
Walks sedately and prim,
Ignores every him
Who whistles a quick invitation;

But the me that I hide
Away down inside
Breaks into a dance
At each masculine glance
And winks at the least provocation!

Wall St. Journal

The Inner Door

Enter, my Friend, thru the inner door
To the room where I do all my dreaming.
Know too, that you are the first, my friend,
To witness its warmth and its gleaming.

Here hide my thoughts more precious than gold
Held safe in their soft, silken wrapping;
Thoughts I had fused from the cold, misty dawn
Or gleamed from the dreams of my napping.

Watch how they crowd at the outer door,
Aroused by their selling and buying...
"New thoughts for old!" and "Down with the old!"
This is the gist of their crying

Here in my inner room we can share
The hopes my soul has of becoming..
Enter, my Friend, thru the inner door..
I have waited long for Your coming!

The Inner Door #2

Enter, my Friend, thru the inner door
To the room where I do all my dreaming.
Know too, that you are the first, my friend,
To witness its warmth and its gleaming.

Here hide my thoughts more precious than gold
Held safe in their soft, silken wrapping;
Thoughts I had fused from the cold, misty dawn
Or gleaned from the dreams of my napping.

Here in my inner room we can share
The hopes my soul has of becoming..
Enter, my Friend, thru the inner door..
I have waited long for your coming!

Beat of wings

Persuasion

I'm three today and Mama says
That if I run away no more
And eat my porridge while it's hot…
That next year I'll be four!

Dearborn Press

Keyboard Notes

My asterisk (*) is sharp and brisk,
My dash (-) is gay and charming;
But oh, the way my poems don't pay
Is really quite alarming!

I cross my T's with silken knees..
My bell is quite compelling
And though my I's are soft and wise..
My poetry's not selling.

My ribbon too is still like new
And so it is disgusting..
For though my space can hold its place
My dollar sign ($) is rusting!

(Note: Mother always used a manual typewriter)

Clair de Lune

When I hear "Clair de Lune" I feel
That everything is blue, unreal!
Dressed in a gown of silver lace
I'm suspended far out in space
Halfway between the earth and sky,
While strange planets go streaking by
Like silver flashes in the night
Then fading slowly from my sight!

(Whispering Wind)

Is It?
Or
My Mother

My mother was a little girl
With dark hair falling free...
A dancing, laughing little girl
Who walked just ahead of me!

Her eyes were full of mischief,
Her hands were never still...
And her merry voice could echo
The thrush or whip-poor-will!

Now I am a mother too...
Yet always I can see
That dancing, laughing little girl
Who walked just ahead of me!

Detroit Times

A Little Boy's Prayer

Now I lay me down to sleep
Mama, do you count the sheep
Like Daddy does? And are they white?
And why do they come just at night?
I pray the Lord my soul to keep
Mama, do little angels weep
When boys like me aren't very good
And do the things they oughta should?
If I should die before I wake
Mama, did you bake the cake
For Daddy like you said you would?
Gee, Mom, your cake is awful good!
I pray the Lord my soul to take
Bless Aunt Marie and Uncle Jake
And Mom and Dad and my white mice
And bless Yourself 'cause You're so nice!

Family Digest

A Little Boy's Prayer (version 2)

Now I lay me down to sleep
Mama, did you see the sheep
The old man across the street
Bought today and does he bleat?
I pray the Lord my soul to keep
Mama, do little angels weep
When boys like me aren't very good
And do the things they oughta should?
If I should die before I wake
Mama, did you bake the cake
For Daddy like you said you would?
Gee, Mom, your cake is awful good!
I pray the Lord my soul to take
Bless Aunt Marie and Uncle Jake
And Mom and Dad and my white mice
And bless Yourself 'cause You're so nice!

Family Digest

Mother

Her day starts with the sun,
She's many people in one.
She's counselor, teacher and clerk,
She's seamstress and farmer;
But still the gay charmer
For she mustn't look like she works!

She's cook and she's baker,
The raggy-doll maker.
She's banker and barber and cop.
She's dispenser of pills,
Consultant for chills,
And when she's not busy… she'll shop!

When her long day is done
And she's tucked in each son
And her baby lies curled in a heap,
Then her time now is hers
Time for diamonds and furs..
BUT ALL SHE CAN THINK OF IS SLEEP!

One More Hill

Always one more hill to climb!
A wise man doesn't hesitate
Or wonder if he has the time.
He goes on with a steady gait!

Just a foolish man would say
When he has reached the peak,
"Now, here forever I will stay.
There's nothing left to seek!"

A man, who has an open mind,
Will climb each hill to see
What new ideas he can find!
I wonder which you'll be?

(Whispering Wind)

The Puzzle

Why is it the pert
Little ladies named Gert
Will fall for the tall, lean Adonis
While sky-scraping gals,
The Patricias and Sals,
Have short, stubby men thrust upon us!

Detroit News?

The Night

When I find tension binds me tight
Then I walk out to meet the night
And share with him my joy and woe,
For he will hold them safe, I know!
No secret do I keep from him:
He knows every hidden whim,
Every thought and fancy dream,
Every little childish scheme,
Every smoldering desire
That could so soon become a fire!
Though he knows all these things of me,
He still remains a mystery!

(Whispering Wind)

Rare Specimen

Let's offer a tribute to Officer Smith,
Patrolling the roads, dry or muddy,
Who never in twenty-one years has said,
"Hey where is the fire, Buddy?"

Detroit News

Apology for Dreams Unwanted

He comes! He comes, this denizen of night,
Unmindful of a wall of brick or stone.
He comes with armor clanking in his flight
And always finds me waiting there alone.

Each dawn, forsooth! I swear this must not be
And gird my covers high with weighty books
And stuff my brain with tepid thoughts of tea,
Old Maiden Aunts, cold sausages and cooks.

Alas, my day-light plans have been for nay.
He comes again with shouts and flashing blade.
How can I send this daring man away…
'Tis but a dream and I am but a maid!

The result of re-reading "Knights of the Round Table" King Arthur,
 Sir Lock….
(Upon seeing "Knights of the Round Table")

The Cynic

My eyes hold a mocking gleam.
I laugh at love.. I'm wise;
But things aren't always as they seem
For my heart cries and cries!

Extinction

A part of me runs out to meet
EVERYONE upon the street.
And let a person call my name..
She can lay a special claim!

Each dog who gives a friendly wag
Wears part of me as his own tag.
Each cat that purrs, each bird I see
Carries off some part of me.

Someday when someone comes to call..
There'll be no ME left here at all!

Enigma
Or
Enigma-Woman

Proud as Queen Kailimai,
Warm as new buttered toast,
Still as the endless tide
That hugs the sun-drenched coast.

Keen as a Caliph's blade,
Soft as a mating call..
Who thinks he knows her best...
Fool! Knows her not at all!

Is There a Baby in the House?
(In reply to the inquiring photographer)

There's diapers blowing in the breeze
And bottles in the sink.
A buggy stands out on the porch..
(I haven't slept a wink).

A teddy bear upon the couch,
A rattle on the floor
And see those tiny fingerprints
All up and down the door?

There's a play-pen in the parlor
That isn't meant for me..
Is there a baby in the house?
Gee, Mister, can't you see?

    Meet the baby. Photographer—You with a chain of safety pins draped across your bosom, standing ankle deep in building blocks.

Dearborn Press
Mother's Home Life

Repentance

The world becomes too much for me
So I hide from its perfidy.
Deep in a wooded glen I run
Till I can hardly see the sun;
Press myself tight against the soil,
And like a cauldron seethe and boil,
Till I am spent!

Like water after too much wine,
Nature soothes this heart of mine,
And rests the aching eyes of one
Who looked too long into the sun.
Shows by her loveliness untold
Which is brass and which is pure gold,
And I repent!

(Whispering Wind)
Dearborn Press

The Chronic Borrower

You sent back the rake and hoe,
My last year's books you borrowed,
My great-aunt's silver tea set,
(A little dent, you sorrowed!)

You sent back my croquet set,
(At least you sent a part)
My tennis racquet, ball and bat..
Now please send back my heart!

Repentance (2)

Beyond the sea of time and space
Where human tides are churning..
Upon a wind-swept barren place
My soul shouts forth in yearning.

"Is there hope for me?" it cries,
A heart in torment pleading.
A muted wind takes up the sighs
And mocks itself receding.

I saw a sudden, misty glow
And heard while still debating..
"Learn ye, as others too shall know..
My child, I'm always waiting!"

Perception

In the sigh of the wind thru the cedars
When the summer night is still..
In the swish of the leaves of the maple
As they brush against my sill..

In the tap of the rain on my window...
In the surging waves of the sea..
You call, and my heart will answer
Wherever I chance to be!

Beat of Wings (Dec. Jan. '48-'49)

Here Lies Hope

Now here lies hope, poor thing! She tried;
But then she kicked her heels and died.
It seems I might as well admit
A twelve again will never fit!

Wall Street Journal

Spectatorship

The game of life is being played
No matter where you're at;
Yet some are born and live and die
And never get to bat!

Some never rise to take a stand
Or plead a free-man's sake,
Or gamble all to right a wrong,
Yet live in freedom's wake.

Some men have struck a blow and lost
Yet thought it worth the try..
Still some there are who come to watch
And some who come to die.

The Wisdom of a Fool

I threw a kiss upon the wind
That raced across the hill.
I followed with a lilting song
A sunbeam from my sill.

I pirouetted with the trees
Beside the quiet pool..
But they had hid inside to watch..
Ah yes, they called me "Fool!"

Detroit News

Inevitable

I must love the flash of lightning
And walking in the rain.
I must harness lively phrases
That go tumbling thru my brain.

I must feel the wind caress me
While time itself holds still
And press myself against the earth
On some secluded hill.

You may never understand me,
Not even if you try..
But these things I MUST do
And love you till I die.

Beat of Wings (Dec. Jan. '48-'49)

Symphony of Sorrow

The night my sorrow is sharing..
Black is the shroud she is wearing..
No moon or stars for my bearing
And I know why!

The wind in the cedars is sighing
And lo, the heavens are crying
For our love lies twisted and dying..
And so am I!

Beat of Wings

Surrender
(Liberache to wed)

Most men are far too bold
To thrill me very much.
My hand is yours to hold..
You have a gentle touch!

These eyes of mine were blind
To thrills they said I'd miss..
How strange that now I find
My lips are yours to kiss!

These years I kept my mind
Have gained me not one sou
For now, alas I find
We're both in love with YOU!

Detroit News

Supply and Demand

The price of tomatoes was way out of sight.
So, I worked and I slaved far into the night
To raise a prize crop, each one red and round,
That you can buy <u>now</u> for five cents a pound!

Dearborn Press

A Portrait of Mother

She set no fashions stirring,
Conceived no current fad;
Yet showed a path to beauty
Blessed by the things we had.

She wrote no lofty music
That critics counted art;
Yet with a further vision
She wrote love in my heart.

She carved no shapeless marble
To some long-sought design;
Yet with a finer sculpture
She shaped this soul of mine.

She sought no worldly claim,
No pleasure paths to trod;
Yet each child at her knee
Met and talked with God.

The Dreamers

They call me a dreamer to haze me,
To tease me as one set apart;
Yet little they know that they praise me
For each wondrous thing, in the start,
Was a dream in some little man's heart!

Yes each bridge, each building and highway
Was a dream in the heart of a man.
Each plane that streaks thru the skyway,
Each ship was a thought and a plan..
A dream held in the heart of a man!

From women, their dreams ever reaching,
Come homes where a forest once stood
And brought from the fruits of their teaching
A nation of people who would
Hold dreams of the right and the good!

Yes, back before time had a measure
Before earth had shadow or span..
God who would share of His treasure
Had a hope, a dream and a plan
He opened His heart and made man!

Wishing

I wish that I were no one
With nothing on my mind.
I'd sail into the setting sun
And leave myself behind.

I'd find a lonely island
Away out in the sea
And spend my time just fishing
And wishing I were me!

Dearborn Press
Detroit News

The Way of a Woman

If I were a queen of rare fascination
I'd offer all the wealth of my nation...
The fabulous bounty of my hidden mines,
A fortune in jewels, rare Burgundy wines...
I'd offer you all, my impetuous knave
To take me and hold me and make me your slave;
But if you refused me, my darling... ah then
You'd never live to see daylight again!

Dearborn Press

Boundaries

This life of mine is bounded by
A cuddly doll with missing eye,
A meerschaum pipe, a fielder's mitt,
A dog collar and an airplane kit!

National Weekly
Dearborn Press

Boundaries (#2)

Each time my heart would run astray
Some little trinket bars my way...
A kewpie doll with broken nose,
A ticket stub, a faded rose,
A snapshot taken at the fair,
The vase we won, a lock of hair,,,

Why is it you can wander free..
And boundaries are just for me?

(Detroit News)

A Poet's Prayer

So I prayed to my Lord.. "Use my voice..
Let me speak for the inarticulate..
For those who weep, the cold and hungry
Who huddle at the outer gate.

For the voiceless, Oh Lord, use my voice.
Let me speak for the burden they bear.
Thru me, let the world hear their suffering.
Thru me, see the rags that they wear.

Use my voice and give it great power..
Not for myself, Oh Lord, do I pray.
Let the world have a better tomorrow
Because I have spoken today."

Westminster Press

Chatter-Box

She has a room in the back of her mind...
The walls from ceiling to floor are lined
With shelves, and stacked in neat little piles
Are empty thoughts in all sizes and styles...

Detroit News

The Point of View

"I'll make my mark," the young man said
With wild and thoughtless boast.
"The world is at the feet of him
Who dares to claim the most!
I'll bend the mountains to my will,
The rivers to my plan.
All men through ages yet to come
Will know I walked with man."

"I've made my mark," the old man said.
"I've built with brick and steel.
The tallest buildings bear my name,
The largest ships, my seal.
I'm tired now," the old man said.
"I'm sick of wars and charts..
Go make your mark on men, my son,
But make it on their hearts!"

Westminster Press

Rendezvous

Anoint my feet with perfume rare,
And let my hair fall free.
My choicest gown of gowns I'll wear..
The soft blue of the sea.

I'm in a restless, searching mood..
A discontented thing.
My other loves I shall elude
And walk away… with spring.

Detroit News

Introspection

I live in my mind, a quiet place,
Tied up with ribbons, patched with lace..
Where day is day if I wish it so
And night always has a moon to glow.

I skip down the alleys, scale the walls..
No one to say I can't run the halls.
I live in my mind, a wide-some place..
With acres and acres of fields to race.

I perch on the limb of the tallest trees
And wiggle my toes at the evening breeze.
So while you're talking of this and that
You never know just where I'm at!

Methodical Mind
Or
Methodical Dreamer

I have a room in the back of my mind.
The walls from ceiling to floor are lined
With shelves, and stacked in neat little piles
Are day-dreams, assorted in sizes and styles!

Dearborn Press

To My Successor

Go ahead and seek, my man!
Comb through the cold dark city,
Find a lassie if you can..
One who's twice as pretty.

Aye, she'll sew a neater seam
And dust in all the corners..
Fill your pipe and share your dreams
And banish all the mourners.

So find a lassie sweet and shy
Who's heart is all forgiving..
But love you, Laddie, more than I
There's not a lassie living.

A Single Mile

If love should saunter past my heart
And beckon with a smile..
With all I have, I'd gladly part
To walk a single mile.

Though love might go at mile's end,
I never would be free.
I'd settle there to wait, my friend.
Love might come back to me!

Beat of wings

A Single Mile

If love should saunter past my heart
And beckon with a smile,
With all I have, I'd gladly part
To walk a single mile.

Although love might go, at mile's end,
And leave me there alone,
The joys I'd found around the bend
Would, for all else, atone.

Though he go journeying afar;
I never would be free!
And so I'd keep my heart ajar,-
Love might come back to me!

(Whispering Wind)

Advice to a Fledgeling
or
The Cynic's Advice

Now I have heard ... in days gone past
There was a man whose love did last
Almost a year...
A rumor, dear!

For ever since the world began
Woman has succumbed to man
And then been left...
Alone... bereft!

So Dearie take this sage advice..
Beware of men and loaded dice!

Dearborn Press

Monochrome

Roses are red...
Violets are blue...
Many colors on the altar...
One color in the pew!

Procrastination

Gay sunbeams streaming thru the door
Make dancing patterns on the floor
While gentle winds that bend the grass
Tap messages upon the glass.

A robin struts across my sill
And weakens more my feeble will...
Tomorrow will be soon enough
To wash and sew and all that stuff!

Dearborn Press
Beat of Wings (Oct. Nov, '48)

Thanksgiving Night!

Matthew, Mark, Luke and John,
Bless the bed that I lie on.
Clear my poor, wine-addled head
And shoo those turkeys off my bed.
Make the mince and pumpkin pie
Quietly within me lie
So mashed potatoes and whipped cream
Will not chase me as I dream!

Dearborn Press

The Worry Wart
Or
The Pessimist

I had a little Worry
The same as each of you...
Yet every time I looked at it,
It grew... and grew... and grew!

It grew so big and fierce and strong,
'Twas horrible to see...
Now everything has turned around...
The worry now has me!

Dearborn Press

Optimist

I took all my little worries
And put them in a box.
I wrapped them with a dozen chains
And used a dozen locks.

I tied it to a great big stone
And tossed it in the sea..
But they, when I returned that night
Were waiting there for me!

Dearborn Press
Detroit News

Pick-Up

It was only a glance but my heart missed a beat,
As I watched for a bus on that crowded street.
He was a little bit short but quite neat and clean;
And he had the darkest eyes that I'd ever seen.
He had curly black hair that my hands ached to comb!
It was love at first sight and no more would I roam.
I could easily see that he felt that way too,
And I knew that his love would always be true.
The decision was made! The boy got a dollar,
And I hooked my leash to the little dog's collar!

Dearborn Press
(Whispering Wind)

Night Cry

Sometimes, when all the world seems gray
With a shadow I can't push away...
When my heart is numb with pounding pain
Like a deep, base drum in driving rain.
When sleep eludes my grasping clutch...
It's then, O Lord, I need Your touch!
To this my watch, my forging time...
Send me a star for my soul to climb!

Anthology of New American Poets

My Secret Ambition

So now, if you'll listen:
My secret ambition
Is to warble a tune like a bird.
When I get the notion
I go thru the motion,
But there's not a sound to be heard!

With all my son's preaching
And his constant teaching,
The most I can get is a "Wheeeee!"
To learn how to whistle
As light as a thistle
Is the height of ambition to me!

(Whispering Wind)

Resolution Time

Each solemn Can and Will and Must
That has been gathering the dust
In some dim corner of my brain
Must be all polished up again.
This year has made some small dents
In vows of even presidents;
But this one thing I must make clear...
I'll do a better job next year.

The Giants Who Walk the Earth

Among the giants who walked the earth,
Whom time cannot erase..
A lanky, simple-hearted man
Has gone to take his place.

With men, who by their very lives,
Have changed the course of fate...
Who rose above the common herd,
The great among the great!

With Edison, who was his friend,
With Washington and Bell,
The simple name of Henry Ford
Must now forever dwell.

These giants who used to walk the earth
Have pointed us the way.
And when we try to carry on...
They walk with us today.

Written upon the death of Henry Ford

Predestination

For a little while, let my hand
Reach out in fright and find you there,
And let my eyes above the crowd
Look in your eyes and know you care!

For a little while, to have to try
To match your lengthy stride to mine
Or trace upon a wind-swept shore
Sand castles of our own design!

From unmeasured distances of time
And space, to grasp this bit of bliss..
To know that we have met and loved,
I ask no more of life than this.

The Turning Point

I've reached the turning point in life,
Alas, my tears remind me...
That whistle wasn't meant for me;
But for the girl behind me!

Detroit News?

Wanderlust

I love you, yet a sailing ship
Full-rigged against the sky
Can fill me with a haunting pain
My heart cannot deny.

I love you.. Yet I hide my head
And hold the covers tight
Because the whistle of the train
Breaks the silence in the night.

Tucked in the corner of my mind,
Upon a busy shelf..
A Gypsy sits and sadly waits
For me to know myself!

Spring

In spring a young man's fancy turns
To ballads of poetic lore..
Each time he sees a pretty girl
It turns like a revolving door!

Detroit News

Advice

Love her, Laddie, while you live...
And sing with joy and laughter!
Kiss her, Laddie, while you live...
It's much more fun than after!

On Growing Old

Some things grow nicer growing old
Like cheese, old books and wine...
Old furniture takes on a gleam,
(Age gives a special shine).

Some folks grow nicer growing old
A pleasure to be near...
To share a bit of friendliness,
To draw a bit of cheer.

Old friends grow dearer thru the years,
More precious now than gold.
I cherish each and every one,
Now that I'm growing old!

The Two of Me

Part of me wants to be practical,
Part of me hasn't a care...
So part of me saves all my money,
And buys a rose for my hair!

Lucky?

As our lips meet in the promise
Of a long, ecstatic kiss...
I wonder where the girl is now
Who taught you all of this!

Regret

I take back all I said to you
In that haste-written letter...
I take back all the names I used,
I've thought of something better!

Detroit News?

Shackled!

The wind is west! I hear it call…
Beyond the house, across the wall.
Like a gay, full gypsy tale…
See it prancing, feel it wail.

Hear it chatter through the pines…
Now it twitters, now it twines.
Like a small enchanting boy
Using thistles for a toy.

Teasing, teasing till it woke
Rustles from the stately oak.
The wind is west, alive and free…
But I, alas, am only me!

Rocking-Chair Judges

So quick to wield a surgeon's knife
To cut into another's life...
So quick to pound the gavel proud
To shout what should not be allowed.

So quick are they, these creatures bold,
To brand this brass, this shining gold...
To shout aloud from their ant-view
"This is the false! This is the true!"

How He must laugh while looking down
To see them play the pompous clown...
From rocky thrones they judge and blot...
They draw the line where God would not!

After reading an Indian story Two Moons in His Moccasins

For Certain People

Now I lay me down to sleep
And pray before I take my ease...
If I should die before I wake...
A segregated heaven, Please!

Mother never could stand prejudice!

Point of View

A little more determination,
A little more pluck.
A little more work,
Men call it luck

Going to Church

Some go to church for observation.
Some go to church for conversation.
Some go to church to wink and nod.
And a few may go to worship God.

The Reluctant Vision

You walk through my dreams,
A vision in white,
Like a mannequin out on parade;
But just when it seems
I could hold you so tight..
You flutter, and sputter and fade!

Wall St. Journal

Prayer Posture

"The proper way for men to pray,"
Said Deacon Lemuel Keyes.
"The only proper attitude
Is down upon his knees!"

"Nay, I should say the way to pray,"
Said Reverend Dr. Wyes.
"Is standing straight with outstretched arms,
With rapt and upturned eyes."

"Oh, no, no, no," said Ellen Stroud,
"That posture is too proud.
A man should pray with eyes fast closed,
And head contritely bowed."

"It seems to me the hands should be
Austerely clasped in front.
With both thumbs pointing to the ground,"
Said Reverend Dr. Blunt.

"Last year I fell in Hodgin's well
Head first," said Cyril Brown.
"With both my heels a stickin' up,
My head a pointin' down,

And I done prayed right then and there...
Best prayer I ever said.
The prayin'est prayer I ever prayed,
A standin' on my head."

Life

They told me that life would be just what I made it.
Life was a picture in scarlet or gray.
I was the painter and none could disclaim it.
Life was a picture to paint my own way.

So I gathered my paints and my easel around me,
Selected gay colors to give it a gleam.
I sketched in a rose and a gay, careless highway,
The same one that beckons me on in my dream.

But other folks came and watched as I painted,
Some of them questioned my ultimate plan.
Somebody mixed all the paint I was using,
Added some blues to my scarlet and tan.

Other folks said that my background was hazy.
My roses are gone. They met the same fate.
And oh, what they did to my gay beckoning highway.
Some thoughtless soul put up a stone gate!

Life is a painting, but no one man the artist.
"No man is an island to stand all alone."
Every man's grief, his laughter, his suffering,
Is mirrored in the painting that I call my own!

Little Talents (for bazaars)
Or
One Woman's Thoughts on Bazaars

I cannot preach a sermon
Or write a gentle song..
But I can plant a flower
To help His Word along.

I can't design a building
Or right a grievous wrong..
But I can knit or purl a bit
To help His Word along.

I cannot paint a sunset
To thrill a gathered throng..
But I can bake a cake or bread
To help His Word along.

My day is filled with gladness..
I hum a little song
Because these humble tasks of mine
Will help His Word along!

The following poem is about a young girl my mom knew who was crippled from birth and died at a very young age. She told me it was one of the hardest poems she ever wrote because each time she worked on it she cried.

Prayer for a Crippled Child

Dear Susan's gone! Her heart is still.
Forgive this sentimental fool,
But Lord, I beg You, if You will…
Break just one tiny little rule.

Give her a dress three yards around,
A yellow rose bud for her hair,
And bright red slippers, satin-bound…
(I know that's not what angels wear).

Then let her leap and bow and twirl…
Just watch her so she doesn't fall
Dear Lord, she's such a little girl…
Never to have walked at all.

(Mother's Home Life)

Time Is a Thief

Time is a thief who walks in the night
And robs all my dreams of amorous delight.
Just when you succumb to my sensitive charm…
He sneaks into my room and rings the alarm!

The Opinionated Male!

Speak of dogs or indigestion,
Mid-day traffic's sad congestion
Or the merits of a certain brand of fizz…
But don't you dare make one suggestion…
For to each and every question…
There'll be two sides, the one that's wrong and his!!!

Haunted!

I think no matter where you go,
You'll find me there.
You'll hear the echo of my step
Upon the stair.

You'll hear my laughter in the wind,
And feel my hand.
Though you may seek another shore,
Another land!

I think no matter how you try
You won't be free…
For in each new love you would choose…
You will find me!

Foolish Pride

My eyes would not glance your way,
My nose was tilted up;
But my heart followed you around
Like a small, begging pup!

Prayer of a Selfish Child

Now I lay me down to sleep,
I pray the Lord my soul to keep.
And if I die before I wake,
I pray the Lord my toys to break
So none of the other kids can use 'em.
Amen.

Understanding Women

I can't see why there is a fuss
About men understanding us!
A thoughtful word, a loving touch,
A compliment can mean so much.
If given with a kiss, one rose
Means more to us than fancy clothes.
Remember too that love has wings
And women live on little things!

Detroit News

Problem No. 612

When my husband comes home with a big kiss,
Is it because he thinks I'm good-looking;
Or is it because a steak big as THIS
Is now in the frying-pan cooking?

It really is hard for a woman to see
And sometimes can be very trying,
When he says, "You look grand!" does he mean me -
Or is it the chicken I'm frying?

I wish they would find a sure-enough way
To perceive when a husband is fooling;
But who cares, when he hands you his pay,
If he stares at the cake that is cooling!

Dearborn Press
(Whispering Wind)

Lost or Strayed

Gee, Mister, have you seen my dog?
He stands about so high
And wags his tail up to his ears
Each time that I go by.

No he wouldn't run away..
Not from me he wouldn't.
It's just .. he sort of lost his way
And went the way he shouldn't.

He limped a little on one foot...
I guess he's sorta lame;
But when I usta call him...
He almost always came!

Get another? Gee I couldn't...
We been pals for more'n a year
And ever since he went away
I got a hurt right here!

Dearborn Press

Lost or Strayed #2

Gee, Mister, have you seen my dog?
He stands about so high
And wags his tail up to his ears
Each time that I go by.

He limped a little on one foot…
I guess he's sorta lame;
But when I usta call him…
He almost always came!

Gee, Mister, help me find him
'Cause I don't see so clear
And ever since he went away
I got a hurt right here!

Delayed Action

Why does the answer to her little dig
Never seem to enter my head
Until she's been gone for an hour or more
And I'm home safely in bed?

Detroit News

As Long As There Are People

There will be one who would not dream
Of riding a train without paying her fare;
But who will enter into marriage
With no idea of adding her share!

There will be one who pleads and begs
For the funds for the Greeks and the Poles,
While her patient husband waits at home
With his stockings studded with holes!

    I found this hand-written in pencil on a work sheet among some other poems.

Once Is Enough

Once riding in old Baltimore,
Heart-filled, head-filled with glee,
I saw a Baltimorean
Keep looking straight at me

Now I was eight and very small,
And he was no whit bigger,
And so I smiled, but he poked out
His tongue, and called me "Nigger!".

I saw the whole of Baltimore
From May until December;
Of all the things that happened there
That's all that I remember!

Almost Perfect

"Almost perfect...but not quite!"
Those were the words of Mary Hume
At her seventh birthday party.
Looking 'round the ribboned room.
"This tablecloth is pink, not white.
Almost perfect...but not quite."

"Almost perfect...but not quite."
Those were the words of grown-up Mary
Talking about her handsome beau.
The one she wasn't gonna marry.
"Squeezes me a bit too tight.
Almost perfect...but not quite."

"Almost perfect...but not quite."
Those were the words of ol' Miss Hume
Teaching in the seventh grade.
Grading papers in the gloom
Late at night up in her room.
"They never cross their t's just right..
Almost perfect...but not quite."

Ninety-eight the day she died
Complaining 'bout the spotless floor.
People shook their heads and sighed,
"Guess that she'll like heaven more."
Up went her soul on feathered wings,
Out the door, up out of sight.
Another voice from heaven came...
"Almost perfect...but not quite!"

Friendship

We share the little joys of life..
The smell of rain, the sound of brooks
The taste of crispy toast and jam,
The sight of rows and rows of books.

These little joys of life we share
As friends, like bright and shiny beads,
Add color to my duller days
And satisfy my simple needs.

Wondering

I often wonder when I see
People who are new to me
Peek at life as if they might
Be afraid to take a bite.
Did they as children, warm and fed,
Eat only centers of their bread?

(Mother's Home Life Household Magazine)

People I Can Do Without
Or
Dislike

I dislike one who shouts, upsetting
Clerks and waitresses, forgetting
That they are people too, complete
With hearts and minds and aching feet!

Dearborn Press

Poems about Love

Communicate, Please!

Darling, if your heart says, love me..
Love me now while I can know
All the sweet and tender feelings
Which from real affection grow.

If your thoughts are sweet, my dear one,
Wont you tell me? Is it wrong
If you know it makes me happy,
Makes my heart break into song?

So then, my darling, if you love me
Show me by your words and smile..
Women are such funny creatures..
We need loving all the while!

Untitled

Dear heart, did you love me deeply
In some strange land or clime?
How could a love grow strong as ours
In only one life-time?

The Hoarder

Love hoards so many things, poor love!
Small trinkets hidden in some dim
Recess of my mind to gather dust
And only aired at some fool whim.

Love hoards, refusing to release
A half-forgotten laugh, a tune
We hummed along a country road,
A faded rose, a dance in June.

A tinseled ribbon from a box,
Our meeting place beneath the tree,
Because I am too practical to try,
Love hoards so many things...for Me!

Freedom

Just like a chain
Around my heart,
Love holds me bound
When we're apart.

Although you're gone,
I can't be free.
Whoever said
I want to be?

Patterns

Here, take my love
And trace a pattern in the sky.
Be sure to show
The golden hours slipping by.

Now draw a house
With many windows filled with light.
Two children dear
And two more hiding out of sight.

Now draw yourself.
(See you haven't lost the touch)
With me right by,
Needing you so very much.

Fate vs. Love

Fate sought to play a trick on love
By taking you away from me.
I begged the heavens up above
To guard you in your destiny.
In the soft wind I heard your voice
Vowing our love would not abate.
Even the stars on high rejoice,
For love has turned the trick on fate!

(Whispering Wind)

If (with apologies to Kipling)
Or

To the New Bride...

If you'll kiss when his chin is lost in the brush
And he's covered with fish-smelly scales,
Or your world, when he sleeps, walks around in a hush..
And you're silent on planning that fails!

If your heart does a pop-up each time he returns
Or turns into wood if he's late..
If you don't mind the cuts, the scratches, the burns
Or the once-a-month hamburger date!

If you fix his best dishes, (the ones you can't eat!)
Or hunt half a day for his glove!
Honey, you've something that money can't beat..
Can't eat it! Can't wear it! It's LOVE!!!

Plea

I must meet life as I really am;
No inhibitions, falsity or sham!
As you love me please try to understand
I will always be a child of the land!
Living your way, my life would be a lie,
And the real me would shrivel up and die!
Can't you see dear, I'll be a loyal wife,
But I must keep my rendezvous with life?

(Whispering Wind)

Love

Love is a maiden,
Sweet and shy,
Who trips your heart
As you pass by.

Love is a maiden,
Fair of face,
Who binds you tight
With a bit of lace.

Love is a maiden,
Soft and round.
Who walks away
And leaves you bound!

Detroit News

These Things I Must Do

I must love the flash of lightning and walking in the rain,
And harness lovely phrases that go tumbling thru my brain;
I must lose myself in music, till I know not the hour;
Press myself against the grass in some secluded bower;
And feel the sun's rays warm me like a lover's soft caress,
In the joy of living find my greatest happiness.
You may never understand me, not even if you try.
But these things I MUST do... And love you till I die!

(Whispering Wind)

Our Love Has Changed

We swore, when sweethearts we became,
Our love would always stay the same!
Fools we were to think we could hold
The first bright flame love's glory told!
This love is not like the first we had;
I'm not sorry, Darling! I am glad!

Where it flamed with but love's desire,
Years have added fuel to the fire!
Where first it was a shining light,
It roars with a forest-fire's might!
This love is not like the first we had;
I'm not sorry, Darling! I am glad!

(Whispering Wind)

Your Name

It's funny what your name can do!
While sitting here, just feeling blue,
I heard your name that someone spoke,
And through the clouds the sunshine broke.
I felt the thrill of your warm embrace;
My hands reached out to touch your face.
Then through my heart a pounding came,-
And all I did was hear your name!

(Whispering Wind)

Just For You

These things would I do for you;
I'd pluck a star out of the blue
And place it in your dark-brown hair.
(It would shine so lovely there.)
If you were mine, I'd be so proud
I'd build a stairway to a cloud
And place you on a golden throne,
Then keep you there to be my own!

(Whispering Wind)

For You

These things would I do for you;
I'd pluck a star from out the blue
And place it in your dark-brown hair.
(It would shine so lovely there.)
I'd gather drops of morning dew
And make a string of pearls for you.
There is nothing I would not do,
If I knew you loved me too!

Love Walked With Me

Love walked with me beside the river,
And my searching heart ached with the pain
Till it could shatter into small bits!

The Ghost of Love makes my heart shiver.
I will never walk alone again;
Always at my side his shadow flits!

(Whispering Wind)

A Kiss

Upon my lips you placed a kiss!
Just like a flaming dart
Its lonely target could not miss:
It shot straight to my heart!

And other fires kindled there
Until in roaring flame
Now, for a heart, a brand I wear
That spells your loving name!

(Whispering Wind)

The Hapless Male

Does my dark hair with reddish lights
Send your heart on ecstatic flights
And do you think my eyes of green
The most enticing you have seen?

When your lips, my dear, touch mine..
Do butterflies run up your spine
And make you long to keep me near?
You say the sweetest things, my dear!

Autumn Song

We meet as strangers chance to meet
Upon a crowded city street
And find it easy to pretend
We never said, "Until the end
Of time, we two, alone shall love!"
When stars were warm and bright above!

One Life

One life is so short a time
To spend with you, my dear..
Walking with your hand in mine,
Thru each succeeding year.

Now, I have been a happy wife;
But this still puzzles me.
If you had another life
Would you live it with me?

Lost

Don't you know I'm lost without you
Like a stray, forgotten sheep?
All those things I loved about you
Even haunt me in my sleep.

Every day is dull and gloomy..
Can't see clearly thru my tears.
Even stars mean nothing to me
And I dread when night-time nears.

A thousand times I've read your letter,
Can't believe all that it means.
Guess I'm not a good forgetter
Keep on clinging to my dreams.

I've no pride where you're concerned, dear..
Let the world think what it will..
There's one thing that I have learned, dear
How I love you… love you still!

Lost #2

Don't you know I'm lost without you
Like a stray, forgotten sheep?
All those things I loved about you
Even haunt me in my sleep.

Don't you know my heart is lonely
Like a glove without its mate.
Can't you tell I want you only?
Is it fair to make me wait?

Other men would do things for me..
Wealthy men, and handsome too.
To tell the truth, they only bore me.
All in this world I want, is you!

Heart-Song

Deep in my heart a gentle beat
Will quicken when I hear your feet
Upon the walk. Thru tear-spun lace
I'll reach my hand to touch your face
And whisper low, "At last, you came!"
My head, so lost till now, will claim
It's place upon your shoulder; seek
Roughness of tweed against my cheek!

Yes, I will weep; but I will wait.
You are my destiny… my fate!

Awakening

I lived! At least I thought I did!
I walked and talked and slept!
I laughed at someone's clever joke
And sometimes even wept;

But then you took me in your arms
And kissed my hungry lips..
The blood rushed from my very soul
And found my fingertips!

I lived; but now I am alive
To every sight and sound..
A pulse I never knew before
Began to pound and pound.

There is a humming in my heart
Like bees around a hive..
I lived, oh yes, I lived before
But now I am alive!

Without Your Love

Dear, life would be a barren thing
Without the warmth your love can bring.
Gray thoughts would crowd my mind
Like sheep;
And they, who read my verse,
Would weep!

Copyright 1946

My Plea

Don't try to call me nightly
(The neighbors might complain)
Or hold my hand so tightly
(I might enjoy the pain).

Don't let your arms enfold me
(Not even if I plead)
Or let your kisses hold me
(Though they are what I need).

And please, don't be the nearest
When stars are bright above.
For can't you see my dearest,
That I'm afraid of love?

The Time Has Come

The time has come when I must go
Along that lonely path and join
The ranks of loves you used to know
While you, Gay Bard, attempt to coin
Phrase to sing the praises of
The lucky one whom, now you love!

Love Offering

I'll try, my dear, each day to bring
Into your life some lovely thing!
A melody the wind has played;
A sunbeam thru the window strayed;
A scalloped leaf; a snowflake bright;
The starlight shining in the night;
And then to make your day complete,
I will sit quietly at your feet
And hold my heart, cupped-fashion so
That you can see the love-light glow!

For All These

For reaching out to hold my hand;
For showing me you understand
When plans of mine have gone awry;
For liking crazy hats I buy;
For sitting up with me when sleep
Eludes me like a frightened sheep;
For being near me when I'm blue,
Each day I fall in love with you!

(Woman's Magazine)
(Whispering Wind)

Late-Night Thoughts!

Do you remember, Love we swore
That when the preacher'd mate us;
No storm that raged no fury caged,
Would ever separate us?

These words led to many things:
Satin ribbons, wedding rings,
Leases and refrigerators,
Apron strings, perambulators.
Cheese and rice and baby shoes,
Shaggy dogs that chew the news,
Teething rings and kiddie cars,
Baseball bats and sudden stars,
Cuts and bruises, measles, mumps,
Coffee cold and gravy lumps...

You're stirring now, some dream perhaps
Of great success or glory.
I'd ask you, Love, had I the nerve..
Are you GLAD.................... or SORRY?

Anniversary Thoughts

So little have I done it seems,
Helped in harvesting your dreams,
Swept the house, scrubbed it through
Little things that all wives do.

So little have I done yet you
Have toiled weary hours through
To cherish us and keep us warm,
Safe and snug against the storm.

Each year a prize, each day a gem..
I would part with none of them.
And pray the future yet but hold
Moments more of this pure gold.

So little have I done, it's true..
Just the things that all wives do..
Sweep the house, wash and mend
And love you till my life shall end.

My Love

My love was a pool
Far from the sea.
To quench your thirst
Was my only plea.

My love was a pool
That was born to die
For you came this way
And passed me by!

Lyrical and Anthology of New American Poets

Choice

Everything or nothing!
No in between for me.
Darling take my whole love
Or let me be.

Everything or nothing!
No half-love will I buy.
Toss away your old love
Or let me die.

Lyrical and Anthology of New American Poets

Lucky

Your silence speaks of many things..
It says our love affair is thru..
But then, I'm luckier than some..
I've known the thrill of loving you!

A Silver Thread

I would not chain you to my side
For love will never chains abide;
But I will weave a silver thread
Instead
To bind you to me!

Light as an angel's kiss would be,
Yet strong as all eternity;
That you are bound, you'll never guess
Unless
You try to leave me!

(Lyrical and Anthology)
(Whispering Wind)

To a Questioning Lover

Don't probe to find the reason
For the soft glow in my heart..
Would you ask the month or season
Why today, it had to start?

Don't seek to prove the fitness
Of the promise in my eyes..
Let my lips alone be witness
That my love wears no disguise!

Beat of Wings

When a Woman Loves a Man

When a woman loves a man,
She needs no rhyme or reason,
She heeds no time or season
When a woman loves a man
As I love you!

When a woman loves a man,
She'll end her way of living
To spend her day in giving
When a woman loves a man
As I love you!

Compensation

Love compensates for many things
The whole world 'round.
Music heard with you beside me
Is more than sound!

Wine quenches, when you share my cup,
Much more than thirst.
And bread with you is more than food
When love comes first!

(Poet's Herald)

Untitled

When you call me darling, or Lovely or Dear,
I'm suspicious that it's just for atmosphere.
And where you were last night is not very clear...
And yet ... and yet ...
How can I forget you, my pet?

Each time you see a girl you flash a silly grin,
The orchids you brought were just for old Aunt Min,
The girl you kissed was an out-of-city kin.
And yet ... and yet ...
How can I forget you, my pet?

I think that you are brutal, conceited and more...
Your ties are atrocious, you probably snore...
You trampled my heart till it's battered and sore...
And yet ... and yet ...
How can I forget you, my pet?

Assurance
or
If

If loving means that you will be
For me the only one
And other men will always be
Just shadows in the sun.

If loving means the world would be
A dark and dismal place
Were you not there to hold my hand
Or share a warm embrace.

If loving means you'll always be
All things both right and true
And nothing can defeat our love..
Then I'm in love with you!

A Woman In Love

Now a woman in love is an unpredictable thing
She laughs when she's in trouble, and cries when she should sing.
She'll tell him to go when she wants him to stay,
Then dies a little in her heart each day that he's away!

Spiritual Poems

The Star Who Ran Away

There was much ado
In the heavenly blue
For a little star ran away.
The poor angels cried
And the south wind sighed;
But she didn't return that day.

They found her at last
With a girl in a cast
Whose body with pain was torn....
The Good Lord forgave
One who didn't behave
Because it was Christmas Morn!

The Star (North Syracuse)

Epitaph for a Poor Rich Man
or
Epitaph

They carved on a stone, above his green sod,
"He had a nodding acquaintance with God!"

(Whispering Wind)

No title

God is a good provider!
He makes our living great...
He gives us lakes to fish in,
But we must dig the bait!

Are We Really Thankful

Today, upon a bus, I saw a lovely girl with golden hair.
I envied her, she seemed so gay, and wished I were as fair.
When suddenly she rose to leave, I saw her hobble down the aisle.
She had one leg and wore a crutch and, as she passed, a smile!
O GOD, FORGIVE ME WHEN I WHINE.
I HAVE TWO LEGS. THE WORLD IS MINE!

And when I stopped to buy some sweets, the lad who sold them had such charm.
I talked with him, he seemed so glad. If I were late 'twould do no harm.
And as I left he said to me: "I thank you. You have been so kind.
It's nice to talk to folks like you. You see," he said, "I'm blind"!
O GOD, FORGIVE ME WHEN I WHINE.
I HAVE TWO EYES. THE WORLD IS MINE!

Later, walking down the street, I saw a child with eyes of blue.
He stood and watched the others play. It seemed he knew not what to do.
I stopped a moment, then I said: "Why don't you join the others, dear?"
He looked ahead without a word and then I knew he could not hear.
O GOD, FORGIVE ME WHEN I WHINE.
I HAVE TWO EARS. THE WORLD IS MINE!

With legs to take me where I go...
With eyes to see the sunset's glow...
With ears to hear what I would know...
O GOD, FORGIVE ME WHEN I WHINE.
I'M BLESSED INDEED. THE WORLD IS MINE!

As A Child

She has a friend, my little lass,
She talks to every day.
He sits with her at table
And runs with her at play.

When illness came on fevered wings
The vigil cup he shared...
She showed him first the robin's nest
Because she knew he cared.

He is her friend. She walks in trust..
No doubts to bar her view..
You cannot know her long before
You find you know Him, too!

Oh Lord, I understand and pray,
"Childlike, let us live this day!"

The Atheist

An atheist is like the man
Who once upon a famous clock did scan,
And gazed upon its carving grand
Of angels on its granite stand;
That had withstood the test of time,
Then shrugged his shoulders, turned to go
And said, "Nobody made it so!"

(Whispering Wind)

Trust

Wisdom walks on children's feet
And dances in their eyes.
The old are cynics tired and beat.
The young are often wise.

They see God in a butter-cup,
In rainbow after rain,
In fleecy clouds while looking up,
In solace after pain.

We people grapple after light
Thru murky depths of fear..
A child's faith is shiny bright..
"I know that He is here."

The Minister

He does not ask for crowds to rise
Or people shout his name..
No world's distinction does he seek,
No churchly pomp or fame.

His church could brick or sandstone be,
His pulpit, pine or oak...
He only prays that they will know
"He lives! Today, God spoke."

I Saw the Hands

The hands of the Savior I've seen
With a touch that was gentle, pure.
And I saw what these hands can mean,
How they try to heal and cure!

Though some came with sadness and shame,
The hands were still gentle and mild.
They treated the sick and the lame;
The old, the new-born and with child!

The hands were tender with pity
Sending pain and fever away.
I saw His hands in this city;
In the hands of a doctor, today!

(Whispering Wind)

Four Things

Four things a man must learn to do
If he would make his record true…
To think without confusion, clearly;
To love his fellowmen sincerely;
To act from honest motives purely;
To trust in God and heaven securely.

My mother has the following as written by Gail Oakley grade 8B5, but much of it was her. Gail Oakley is, of course, me. However, I am certain I didn't have the skill to write this alone. It was probably an assignment I had that caused me to go to her for help.

Litany of Thanksgiving #3

For all things right,
For day and night,
For blessed sight,
We thank thee, Lord!

For summer rain,
For hands and brain,
For friends we gain,
We thank thee, Lord!

For schools and books,
For trees and brooks,
For shady nooks,
We thank thee, Lord!

For plants that grow,
For winter snow,
For stars that glow,
We thank thee, Lord!

For clothes we wear,
For clean fresh air,
For love we share,
We thank thee, Lord!

For joy and mirth,
For Jesus' birth,
For all the earth,
We thank thee, Lord!

The Christmas Spirit Comes to Our House

I was caught up in the dizzy whirl
Of buying gifts for boy and girl;
Of packages to wrap up tight
And lights to shine out in the night;
Of sorting out the Christmas ties
And baking all the luscious pies.

Then, we picked out the manger site
And each one helped to make it right.
The Baby, on the hay will lie
With silent Joseph standing by
And Mary in her mantle blue.
The sheep and angels are there too!

I begin to feel a peace within
As someone else suggests a hymn.
The holly wreaths and lighted trees
Are far away, as on our knees,
The offering of a song we bring
To worship Him, the new-born King!

(Whispering Wind)

The Shadow of the Cross

I saw it standing, gaunt and tall,
Against a cloud-filled sky.
Its begging arms were open wide.
How could I pass it by?
But I am weak and so I turned
A deaf ear to its plea.
Now every place I seem to go,
His cross precedeth me!

I saw it from a busy street
And from a country lane,
The shadow of His lonely cross,
The sign of grief and pain.
I can't escape its pleading arms.
"Come ye, and follow me!"
No matter where I seem to go,
His cross precedeth me!

The shadow of His cross I see,
The cross by sorrow lined,
And when I close my aching eyes,
I see it in my mind.
Yes, even in my darkened room
I hear its silent plea!
"Oh Lord, my life is yours to take,
Your cross precedeth me!"

Perspective

When I am tired unto tears
And feel, in age, a hundred years,
Then all my tiny little fears
Assume the aspect of a dark, depressing cloud!

But, when my poor body's rested
Of my fears, I seem divested.
With God's help my doubts I've bested,
And with renewed faith and courage I am endowed!

(Whispering Wind)

Alive

Oh, Lord, Master; heed my prayer!
For this I'll always strive:
How long I live I do not care
But let me stay alive!

(Whispering Wind)

A Mother's Prayer

There are things in life I must do!
Oh, help me, Lord, to see them through.
This mother's work will be for naught,
Teach I not what You want them taught!
Help make them good and loyal; kind,
With open heart, tolerant mind;
And for their daily life a creed
To help them meet their every need!

(Whispering Wind)

The Sick Child

An atheist sat by the bed of his child
Whose voice, in her fever, was thick and wild.
Putting her moist hand to his cheek he cried
And thought of God Whom he'd boldly denied.
And then in a voice that quivered and broke,
To his God, Creator, Redeemer, he spoke!

(Whispering Wind)

Adoration

My heart had been sorely troubled,
Filled with vague unrest,
So I climbed a lonely hillside
Up to its ragged crest.
I felt like a kindred spirit
To dark clouds moving by,
Then I saw that they were building
A cathedral in the sky.
Now the windows were all lighted
By the moon, bright as day,
And little stars arranged themselves
For they had come to pray.
Swaying trees began an anthem
And as the volume grew,
Even the wind picked up the chorus
And carried it on through.
It spoke to my heart of glory
And adoration. Then
A long, low roll of thunder
Gave out a loud "Amen!"
Then gentle rains came from heaven,
Washed away my despair
As I knelt and worshipped with them
Upon that hillside there!

(Whispering Wind)

A Christmas Star

A Christmas star came down to earth.
A star that hailed a baby's birth.
But what a babe! The world stood still!
Both God and man, psalms to fulfill!

Maker of all... great God above...
Sent down his Son to us ... with love!

What Is It All?

What is it all, when all is told,
This constant striving for fame or gold,
The fleeting joys, the bitter tears,
We are only here a few, short years.
Nothing our own but the silent past,
Loving or hating, nothing can last!
What is it all but a passing through,
A cross for me, and a cross for you.
Ours seems heavy while others' seem light
But God, in the end, makes all things right!
He tempers the wind with much loving care,
He knows the burdens each can bear...
Then He changes life's gray into heavenly gold,
Oh, that is all, when all is told!

Walls

The walls of Jericho fell down,
The walls of Troy laid low
And thus, if man is to survive,
The walls of fear must go.

No trumpet blasts assault the sky,
No drums announce their end.
God puts your darker hand in mine
And says "Behold, a friend."

Westminster Press

There Is Never a Day So Dreary

There is never a day so dreary but God can make it bright.
And unto the soul that trusts Him, He giveth songs in the night.
There is never a path so hidden but God will lead the way.
If we seek for the Spirit's guidance and patiently wait and pray.

There is never a cross so heavy but the nail scarred hands are there,
Outstretched in tender compassion, the burden to help us bear.
There is never a heart so broken but the loving Lord can heal,
For the Lord that was pierced on Calvary doth still for His loved
    ones feel.

There is never a life so darkened, so hopeless and unblest,
But may be filled with the light of God and enter his promised rest,
There is never a sin or sorrow, there is never a care or loss,
But that we may bring to Jesus and leave at the foot of the cross.

Sudsy Thoughts

Bubble, bubble, toil and trouble!
Break a cup and make it double!
Soapsuds swirling round and round
Wash away each angry sound
Wash needless pain and hateful hurt
Right down the drain with other dirt.

The world could use a lot of soap
To shine its faith and scour its hope!

Christian Home Magazine
The Star (North Syracuse)

The Voice of God

I do not know how this can be.
But I do know, He speaks to me!
Don't ask me how or even why.
I can't explain it if I try.

I only know.. The flame is lit
And I am just a part of it.
Yet reflected in that glow
Every child I teach will know!

Westminster Press

The Least of These

He spoke to those at the grinding wheels,
To the sailor who goes to sea..
He speaks in a voice, so low and clear..
"What have you given for me?"

He spoke to those of the mid-day rush,
To the woman who shops for bread,
"My people are hungry and cold tonight..
How have you helped?" He said.

He pleads with us to share what we have
With those who have less than we.
"Whatever you give to them, my child,
So then have you given to me!"

Heaven

What can a wise man know of heaven?
How could he know what path to trod?
Let a trusting child lead him,
Stumbling, faltering up to God

Heaven (2)

Along the wall where Peter stands
Are marks of tiny, chubby hands
And I'm sure you'll find some more
All around the Outer Door!

The windows of the sky are steamed
By childish faces, freshly gleamed
And little angels slip in late
Scratching up the Pearly Gate.

I haven't seen it, yet I know
'Cause He loves little children so!

Mother Mary

Mother Mary, did you smile
As he slept with fingers curled,
Knowing, wisely, all the while
He was Savior of the world?

Mother Mary, did you guess
As He toddled to your knee,
All too soon these feet would press
Up the path to Calvary?

Mother Mary, did you bind
Each tiny bruise with loving care,
Knowing in your heart you'd find
A pain, someday, too much to bear?

The Master's Plan
Or
The Master Plan

There are plans to be made for a peaceful world
And each shares a part in the plan.
Their children to feed, the aged in need,
Regardless of country or clan.

There are battles to fight for a peaceful world,
(The good never comes without cost).
Fear must be fought and hunger and pain
If freedom is not to be lost.

We must bind the wounds of a battered world,
And help them to bury their dead.
For show me a man who can pray to his God
When his children are starving for bread.

Untitled

We mutter, we sputter,
We fume and we spurt.
We mumble and grumble,
Our feelings get hurt.
We can't understand things,
Our vision gets dim..
When all that we need
Is a moment with Him.

Reflections

There are no stars reflected in this lake..
Small, fragile half-thoughts still unsaid;
Soft half-formed dreams each one must soon forsake,
The hunger of man's heart yet still unfed.

No stars, but memories of tears not shed,
A prayer breathed by a child yet unborn.
Dark are the waters of this timeless bed
By aeons swirled to form then be re-torn.

Deep as the mind of him who somehow dares
To trace the past in surf upon the sand
And finds the outline of the One who cares
And moves each ripple with a master's hand.

Oddities

How odd
Of God
To choose
The Jews.

But odder still
Are those who choose
To choose the God
Who chose the Jews

Anonymous

Who am I? No one you would know..
Why you would pass me on the street
And never glance my way;
Yet God created light for me,
A world in which to stay.
The right to live.. to think.. to grow!

Who am I? No one you'd recall.
Yet God made rivers broad and deep
In which to cool my feet.
He made tall trees with lofty boughs
To shield me from the heat;
He gave me winter.. spring.. and fall.

Don't ask my name! Ask them instead
If I have used these eyes to see
The need upon the land.
Or used my heart to share its grief..
Or lend a helping hand..
Ask them if I have shared my bread!

Westminster Press

POEMS ABOUT WORK

My mother worked in the Edison Junior High lunchroom in Dearborn, Michigan. When she moved to North Syracuse, New York, she went to work for the Cicero High School Lunchroom. These were written about the women on the lunchroom staff.

To the Lunchroom Girls!

There's an extra special something..
Just a certain kind of flair..
'Bout the girls who make the lunches
You notice when you're there.

They give a short and cheery greeting
To each person when they meet;
But their fingers keep a flying
And they never miss a beat.

Sure, a smile is always ready
Tho' the feet may burn and ache.
She's as neat and clean a picture
As the sandwiches she'll make.

When the serving day is over
And each counter's gleaming bright..
Then she leaves her job, contented..
For she knows she did it right!

Patience, Please

He's small now, with just a dime
And he's taking up your time!
You have a million things to do
And a dime won't see you thru.

Be careful what your features tell
For it's the lunchroom you must sell.
Perhaps before the week will end
He'll bring a quarter and a friend!

On the Lunch Line
Or
On the Line

What if his eyes are blue or brown,
Or if his socks are falling down,
Or if his hair could use a comb,
We'd rather he eat here than home!

What if his grammar's not the best,
His hands won't pass a beauty test,
His trousers sure could use a mend...
You'd better smile cause he's your friend!

Nila was my mother's boss when she worked in the Edison Junior High School lunchroom.

A Tribute to Nila

There are some who carry life's burdens..
(And some have much more than their share)..
With head high, heart full of courage..
And yet when you need them, they're there!

How often we'd come with our problems..
Just begging a chance to be heard.
So she'd set aside all of her worries
And make things right with a word!

She would offer a shoulder to lean on
If sickness or troubles came near..
Yet let your youngster win honors..
She's right in beside you to cheer!

And remember her message at Christmas..
It showed just how truly she cared.
And lest we get wrapped up in getting..
She would gently coax us to share!

We knew that someday she'd leave us
And yet it is hard now to smile..
God bless you and keep you dear Nila..
And think of us once in a while!

These two poems are about the Lunchroom at Cicero High School in North Syracuse, New York. Cicero High serviced three counties (I think). The lunchroom staff was quite large. Jackie was a family friend whose husband worked with my dad and transferred to the North Syracuse plant with my dad when the Detroit plant shut down.

Kitchen Kapers

Now meet the gang at Cicero High..
A bunch that can't be beat!
We fix the food for all the floors
For all the kids to eat!

Now Pauline is our manager
Who welcomes all aboard.
Her secret wish is for a phone
With eighty-four foot cord!

Madeline sees the funny side..
(Not like us somber folk!)
Where is she now? She's gone to see
A man about a joke!

Now Maria cooks the turkeys
And when her work is done
She hurries to her roadside stand..
Sells 'taters by the ton!

Louise is in a frenzy with
A dozen things to bake!
And someone took the cookies,
They should have taken cake!

Now Glad is counting sandwiches—
(She's counted them all twice)
While Mary says the dinner's fine..
Just add a little rice!

Dear Santa Claus, put in your bag.
(Before she is a wreck)
For Theresa dear, some plastic gloves
That fasten 'round the neck!

Now Marion is Boss on Main..
A stimulating chore!
She says if we should misbehave
She'll send us up to Four!

The whole world's helping Charlotte
To find another mate.
But she likes the way she lives.
Keeps giving them the gate!

While Vi, she's of a different mind
She thinks it would be fun!
Her only trouble is deciding..
Must there be only ONE!

Now Jackie is so full of life..
She likes to GO—and bake..
Let someone mention luncheon..
"I'll come! I'll bring the cake!"

Ann tries to help with salads
With fingers crossed for luck
'Cause Pauline said, "Take to the stairs!
The elevator's stuck!"

Now Sophie's making sandwiches,
"Do better on this batch!
I've told you girls a hundred time,
The corners have to match!"

Now Mabel says the food is good..
She's tasted all in sight.
Her diet wasn't meant for here
She hasn't lost a mite!

A clock is what our Barbara needs..
One with an extra hour!
For when she should be on the job
She's still in the shower!

Her husband travels all the time
While Irma sits at home..
She's looking for a second job
To pay the telephone!

Now Peggy does as she is told,
Won't grumble or complain!
I'll never tell a soul that she
Takes turkeys on a plane!

Jan's husband is a railroad man.
She polishes and waits!
Her future job is waiting there..
She'll polish pearly gates!

Now Linda raises dogs for show!
It is a sight to see
How she puts them thru their paces
When each weighs more than she!

Now Bernie serves upon the line.
A smile for you and me.
She's really glad she has two hands
And swears she could use three!

While our Pat's in such a hurry
To make it to her job
She broke a little speeding law!!!
It cost a pretty bob!

Someone straighten Winnie out!
Go out and bring her back!
She's selling "skettie" by the yard
And cookies by the sack!

Then Ruth hits the panic button..
"What's this I'm being fed?
Where's my glasses? Where's my glasses?"
They are right upon her head!

Drowsy Leah yawns and whispers,
"My grandkids I will keep
If Santa Claus will bring me
A pocketful of sleep!"

Now we have some green ones..
Some young, some stiff, some old!
Just send them up to Mary Luke..
She'll make them fit the mold!

Now Eileen was a transplant
From the other High to here.
Some days she thinks she's sorry..
Some days she wants to cheer!

Things changed a lot when Charlie came..
He was so calm and mild.
Now he grumbles and he mumbles..
His harem drives him WILD!

Now our Dick is mighty helpful..
Just a real peachy saint!
But when you really need him bad,
That's where our Dickie AIN'T!

Then Fred comes tearing down the hall,
(Grabs a sandwich as he goes)
"Wake up! Wake up! The Colonel's here!
Chin up! Get on your toes!"

We miss Louise who left us..
A drop-out to be sure.
While Barbara has been missing..
She's out to take the cure!

Here the sounds of suds and fury!
"Too many pans to do!!!"
We don't even check the menu
Until the day is through!!

Lunchroom Ladies

There's an extra special something,
Just a certain kind of flair,
About the girls at Cicero High..
You notice when you're there.

They give a short and cheery greeting
To each person when they meet…
But their fingers keep a-flying
And they never miss as beat.

Sure, a smile is always ready
Though the feet may ache and burn..
Today she'll give a helping hand.
Someday it will return!

There's something you can't measure..
The spirit of the corps!
But everyone can notice it
When they walk in the door!

Prose

Grandma Ann bowled on three leagues and was the captain of two when she was in her 70's. And she traveled all the time with her senior group. I have to believe this is about her.

Where Has Grandma Gone?

Time was when Grandma retired to her rocking chair in the corner and the click-click of her knitting needles was all you could hear. Sometimes she would peer over her glasses, shake her head, and murmur softly "Tish tish" at the antics of the younger generation. Poor, old Grandpa took up his post on the back stoop with his 'chaw' of tobacco and a sharp whittling knife, ready to spend his remaining years fashioning animals for the grandchildren. This was it! The dropping off place to oblivion! Not much to look forward to but Cambric Tea, a hot water bottle and a few kind words.

But not any more! Now Grandma is a gay girl who's more up on the latest Samba steps than a knitting pattern and whose daring hats draw envious glances and are a product of her own creation. Grandpa's tools are gathering dust while he struts out wearing the tie his son thought was too bold and smelling sweetly of some of his grandson's 'irresistible' shaving lotion. It's off for the day to some delightful place, rolling down the highway in a magic chariot filling the air with rollicking music. Don't look now, but the couple in front is holding hands and who knows... there may be a wedding soon. If it's not a bus trip, perhaps it's a play, with Grandma, in ankle sox, playing a convincing Baby Snooks while Grandpa stutters and plays the bad little boy who put gum on the teacher's seat. Or perhaps some of the more lucky ones, who have just returned from a bus trip to Florida, New Orleans or Quebec are anxious to show their fascinating slides.

My hat's off to you! I don't know you by name, but I love reading about your clubs and your travels. Your zest for living is a true inspiration to the rest of this musty, stodgy world. Please don't ever think of yourself as old. You've just been young an awfully long time! God Bless you!

The Queer People (A Short Story)

Patrick McGinnis, five years and twenty-one days of age, flung open the kitchen door and strode determinedly across the yard, His jutting jawline gave warning to any hen brash enough to cross his path. He turned the corner by the barn and took one leap, which ended smack in the middle of the mud-hole reserved for Mrs. Pig and her offspring. The mud was sloppy and cool; but the thrill was gone. He wiggled his toes to let the slimy mass ooze between but the satisfaction which usually flooded his small frame at this, his favorite gesture of defiance, was conspicuously absent.

People! He muttered to himself as he headed down the lane where the dust clung to the wet mud and made his footprints like a giant's. People! He tried hopping on one foot to confuse anyone who might be following him. You never knew what they were going to do next!

He plunged into the ditch at the side of the road and riddled his imaginary adversary with bullets from his old reliable.. the same rifle with which he shot buffalo and tigers in Africa. Having rid himself of his enemy, he scurried to the top of the hill and, making binoculars with his fingers, examined the white school house which nestled in the cove of pine.

It was recess and he could see small figures racing back and forth in a game of tag and probably calling each other glamorous names like Stinky or Slim. Mom couldn't understand a man's need for the common touch... the sense of belonging to the gang.

"Patrick McGinnis was good enough for your father and his father before him and it's good enough for you... Butch indeed!" she had said.

"That's just what I mean," said Pat to the squirrel who eyed him discreetly from a low limb. "People... they just don't understand."

Perspiration curled his dark hair in damp ringlets on his forehead and pressed his thin shirt tight against his warm back. He took it off and tied it around his waist. As he twisted around to examine the effect, he saw old Mr. Stanskowski painting the fence in front of his small, neat house. An old straw hat sat on his head which wore a fringe of hair just above the ears, and his bristly beard kept time with his paint brush. Pat skimmed down the hill and crept closer, commando fashion on his belly, to where the old man was painting.

Pat was filled with pride at his courage. Boy! How he wished the kids could see him now!

Everyone was afraid of old Mr. Beard, as they called him. Even his folks had ordered him to stay away from there and when he had asked why, they just said the Stanskowski's were queer. The boys all teased Mr. Beard by throwing rocks at his chicken house just to hear him rattle of unintelligible phrases in a guttural tone.

Pat crept closer. Mr. Beard wore no shirt under his bib overalls and his dark hair lay like a mattress on his chest and covered his large arms. Just then he caught sight of Pat lying in the weeds and bellowed, "Now you get out of here or I'll... I'll paint your nose green." Pat leaped to his feet and scurried back up the hill like a frightened rabbit and lay panting in the high weeds. He was frightened right down to his toes and it felt exhilarating.

When the thrill had subsided, he rolled over and tried to fix a hex on the old man by squinting his eye and pointing his finger; but he had forgotten the words. Just wait until he told the kids how Mr. Beard had threatened to paint his nose green; but would they believe him?

Maybe having a green nose wouldn't be too bad. Of course, his mother would scold and his sister would probably faint. Girls were such sissies anyway! Maybe then he would just run away and join the circus.

He conjured visions of himself as the star attraction... riding a lumbering elephant down the streets of the city while the boys all ran alongside and cheered him.

Pat slipped gingerly down the hill and approached the old man cautiously, with both fingers crossed behind his back just in case. Mr. Beard looked up and growled "What do you want now?" Pat gulped twice before he found his voice, "Will you please paint my nose green like you said you would, Mr. Beard?"

The old man let out a bellow that made Pat jump before he realized it was laughter... laughter that rolled out in giant waves across the meadow... that made the bristly beard do a polka and the large frame heave up and down.

Pat watched, fascinated. This was better than a side-show. The old man took out a gay bandana from his back pocket and wiped the moisture from his eyes. Then he blew his nose with a bellow like a charging bull. Rubbing his massive hands over his beard, he exclaimed, "So that's what they call me... Mr. Beard..."

Just then the front door opened and his wife stuck her head out. "What's amatter, Johann? Did the bull get loose again?" Mr. Beard nudged Pat so hard he almost fell, and chuckled, "Now I am a bull...See Anna, look we have company. Does he not look like Trina's boy?"

Anna came down the steps, wiping her hands on her apron and looking Pat over carefully.

"Yes he does look like the picture she sent us... a little difference in the eyes and maybe the chin; but almost like it. Would you like some sausage and apple strudel, little boy?"

Pat hesitated for a moment. Then he realized that his small frame consisted of mostly hollow stomach.

The Kitchen was filled with the wonderful odor of hot apple strudel, fresh from the oven. Pat ate until his stomach pressed against his belt. He drank thick buttermilk from a large earthen cup, the likes of which he had never seen before. It was Johann who noticed that Anna was not eating.

"Anna, do you not feel well?" he asked worriedly. She wiped her eyes with the corner of her apron, "It is so nice to have company again, Johann. In the old country we always had many friends, but here..." Her voice broke.

When they had finished eating she took Patrick by the hand and led him into the parlor, where pictures paraded across the mantle like in a procession... Johann and Anna, stiff and formal, in their wedding clothes. The children, eight in all, each in his place of honor; and last of all, Trina's boy whom they had never seen.

Pat watched her while she studied the pictures and the lump in his throat swelled until it hurt like a pain. I must have eaten too much, he thought; but he knew it wasn't true. He quickly reached up and kissed her on the cheek right near her odd-shaped earrings and then ran from the house.

At the gate he turned and looked back. She was standing at the door and smiling. He waved with his hand, making a mental promise to come back often. Then a frown creased his forehead. He couldn't let his folks know. People! They just didn't understand! In fact, people were queer.

Ban the Budget

Now we are three…my husband, Budget and me!

To a girl who was raised in a family where Budget was a dirty word whispered behind closed doors, this can be a traumatic experience! So I've been doing some research on the care and feeding of Budgets. Budgets can be all things to all people. To some, it rates as a majestic potentate in whose direction the whole family salaams every first of the month! Yet I met one cheerful spinster who chortles in life gleefully with only three items in her Budget: Rent, food and miscellaneous. And I'd like to borrow her miscellaneous for just three days! I guess I take after my Great Aunt Pearl who disowned two of her children because she never learned to count past ten.

I strongly suspect that somewhere in my tender, impressionable youth, I must have been frightened by an improper fraction. I am also irrevocably convinced our Budget is a she! No male could resist my advances as she does! No matter how I toss the figures around, it never comes up "Channel no. 5". I have tried everything! Once I even turned the lights down low, put my fingertips lightly on her leather cover and whispered in a deep sepulchral voice:
"Budget, Budget. Tell me pray
Can I have that hat today?"
And the answer came back in a dry, mirthful tone,
"Lady, Lady on your head,
A bucket would look good instead!"

But just let my husband walk in, Throw together a few numbers like our address, his shirt size and my right age, and she hands him a three-day fishing trip and a box of ten-cent cigars.. the hussy!

But just you wait! The women in my family don't give up easily. Wait until the first week in June when the baby SHE said we couldn't afford starts stretching her covers with bills for diapers and buggy covers.

Will she be surprised! Maybe she can give him fishing trips or good cigars; but only I can give him a son!

Woman's Magazine

A Christmas Tribute to Dad

Dads are men with two legs, two arms, one hat, one collar and a headache.

They differ from bachelors in that their headache does not come from wine, women and riotous living, but from worry over telephone bills, the price of beef, and Junior's braces. Dads can be easily recognized by their fish stories, receding hairline and perpetually harassed expressions.

Dad's shoulders wear a slouch from being crouched too long in odd corners of the basement while the younger generation or the Ladies Club holds forth in the parlor

Dads are very handy around the house for replacing broken window panes, carrying out the ashes and hanging pictures.

They are indispensable for little items such as paying bills at the first of the month.

One night a year he attends a stag party at the lodge, getting home with the milkman and feeling more like the milkman's horse which makes him a cad and a reprobate.

For the past few months dad has been a new man or renovation of the old. He has paid off the final installment on the 1950 Christmas bills and his last atrocious tie has found its way into Junior's closet.

He is free to smoke a ten-cent cigar and tip the blond waitress 15 cents without looking over shoulder for the bill collector

BUT

Coming events are already casting their dark shadows before them:

Mom is already trying to decide whether to give Gramps the china cuspidor with the blue, hand-painted forget-me-nots or another hand-knitted scarf to round his collection.

So... as Christmas approaches, the season of happiness and good cheer, let us consider Dad this year and solemnly swear not to buy anything he won't be able to pay for, at least, by April's Fool's day.

Thank You

Detroit News "This Week"

A Prayer on Growing Older

O Lord, thou knowest I am growing older! Keep me from closing my eyes to this fact! Keep me from becoming a pest, a self-appointed sage with a fatal habit of thinking I must say something on every subject. Keep me from the temptation of trying to straighten out everybody's affairs!

Make me thoughtful, not moody; helpful, not bossy. Keep my mind free from the recital of all my experiences in endless detail. Seal my lips about my chain of aches and pains! Teach me to admit that sometimes I am mistaken.. just a little bit! Make me more considerate of others as my age progresses. Let me never grow old.. only older! Lord, if You will help me do these things, perhaps others will find me a joy to be around.

Amen

I Must Go Shopping

One of these days, I must go shopping! I am completely out of self-respect. I want to exchange some self-righteousness I picked up the other day for some humility which they say is less expensive and wears better. I want to look at some tolerance, which is being used for wraps this season.

Someone showed me some pretty samples of peace. We are a little low on that and one can never have too much. And, by the way, I must try to match some patience that my neighbor wears. It is most becoming to her, and I think it might look well on me.

I might try on the little garment of long-suffering they are displaying. I never thought I wanted to wear it, but I feel myself coming to it. Also, I must not forget to have my sense of appreciation mended, and look around for some inexpensive every-day goodness. It is surprising how quickly one's stock of goodness is depleted.

A Housewife's Psalm

The Lord is my Master. He provideth for my real needs. He scrubbeth away the fears of my mind and aireth my soul to the bright sunlight of His wisdom. He sweepeth my sins into the bins of the past and polisheth my life to shine as a mirror, reflecting His goodness and mercy to the world. Yea, though I am depressed by my weaknesses, His strength will carry me. His peace and understanding will cover me like a blanket and I will be fed at the fountain of His mercy forever.

A Student's Psalm

The Lord is my teacher, from Him will I learn all that is right and good. He addeth peace and beauty to my life and subtracteth the sins of my foolishness. He divideth goodness and mercy with people in all places. He multiplyeth my blessings and spelleth out the way in which I should go. He feedeth my soul on His everlasting love and His angels guardeth my sleeping hours. Yea, though temptations are around me, I will not fail, for He walketh beside me. His strength and His wisdom warm me like a cloak and I have made my reservation in the house of the Lord.

(Written by her fourth grade class)

What's in a Word

I used to think I was poor. Then they told me it was self-defeating to think of myself as needy, so I was deprived. Then they told me deprived was bad image, so now I was under-privileged. Then they told me under-privileged was overused, so now I was disadvantaged. I still don't have a dime, but I have a great vocabulary!

Ten Free Gifts for Christmas

These gifts won't cost you a dime, but when you give one of them, you will give the most priceless gift.. YOURSELF!

1. The gift of listening.. One of the greatest gifts we can give to another person is to <u>listen</u> to him. And you must really LISTEN, no interrupting, no daydreaming.. just listen.

2. The gift of signs of affection.. Be generous with your hugs, kisses, and gentle squeezes with the hand. Don't forget the mostly forgotten, pat on the back. They are worth their weight in gold.

3. The gift of a note. Put your little notes where they will surprise those special people.. in her lunch, on her dresser. Send a note to someone who helped you long ago.. a teacher, a neighbor, a friend. Though the note may be a surprise, the message will be pure Christmas.

4. The gift of laughter. Everyone likes to laugh and sometimes we get too busy. Just cut out a cartoon, clip a joke, a riddle. Your gift will say, "I love to laugh with you."

5. The gift of a game. Most people have at least one game they like to play, like Rummy or Checkers. Offer to play your loved one's favorite game. Even if you lose, you'll be a winner because you have shared an experience.

6. The gift of a favor.. Help with the dishes, bake someone's favorite cookies. This gift is more valuable when it anticipates a request rather than responds to one.

7. The gift of a cheerful disposition. Try to be cheerful. That means no complaining, no feeling sorry for yourself, no pessimistic predictions. Your cheerfulness can be a special surprise to a clerk or a mailman or a paper boy.

8. The gift of leaving alone. There are times in our lives when we want nothing better than to be left alone. Become more sensitive to this mood in others.

9. The gift of a compliment. A simple "You look good in blue." Or "I like your hair that way." Can be invaluable to someone who is bushed by the Christmas hassle.

10. The gift of prayer. Pray for everyone on your list. Praying for someone is a way of saying "You are so special to me I often talk to God about you."

These ten gifts will make your Christmas too.

Litany for Thanksgiving

For loving us even when we have turned our back on you,
    We thank you Lord.
For seeking us even when we have not looked for you,
    We thank you Lord.
For guiding us most carefully when we are sure we can find our own way,
    We thank you Lord.
For giving us tasks we neither want nor care to do,
    We thank you Lord.
For seeing us as children when we see ourselves as masters of our own lives,
    We thank you Lord.
For being present even when some men deny you even exist,
    We thank you Lord.
For giving us blessings that remind us after all, that we are only human beings,
    We thank you Lord.
For all these things,
    We thank you Lord.

Litany of Thanksgiving #2

Come, let us thank the Lord for his generous gifts.
For seeing eyes and hearing ears,
> We thank you Lord.

For tasting tongues and arms to fling,
> We thank you Lord.

For voices to sing and shout aloud,
> We thank you Lord.

For toes to wiggle and lips to purse,
> We thank you Lord.

For hard teeth to crunch apples and a tongue to lick with,
> We thank you Lord.

For elastic lungs, inhaling and exhaling,
> We thank you Lord.

For hips to spin hoola-hoops,
> We thank you Lord.

For legs that take us where we want to go,
> We thank you Lord.

For all the parts of our wonderful bodies,
> We thank you Lord.

Amen.

An Easterner's letter to her son

Dear Stanley,

I write to let you know I am still alive. I am writing slowly as I know you don't read fast.

You won't know the house when you come home… we moved.

We had trouble moving, especially the bed. The man wouldn't let us take it in the taxi and we were afraid we might lose your father.

Your father has a nice job and is very responsible. He has about 500 people under him. He cuts the grass in a cemetery.

Our neighbors, the Browns, started keeping pigs. We got wind of it yesterday. Your Uncle Dick drowned last week in a whiskey vat at the distillery. Four of his work mates dived in to save him, but he fought them off bravely. We cremated his body the next day and just got the fire out this morning.

I went to the doctor with your father last week. The doctor put a small glass tube in my mouth and told me not to open it for ten minutes. Your father wanted to buy it from him. It rained only twice last week, once for three days and once for four. Monday it was so windy, the chicken laid the same egg four times. I got a letter from the undertaker this morning. He said if we don't make up the installment on your grandmother's grave, up she comes.

Your loving mother, Stella

p.s. I was going to send you $10, but I had already sealed the envelope.

Songs

Mom's oldest sister, Grace Ruff, played the piano and wrote the music to the songs found in this book. I have tried to track down this music, but have been unsuccessful. I wanted to add the music here, but my Aunt Grace is also deceased and her daughter hasn't found it. This first song was actually cut on a 78 rpm record.

Quit Messin' Around With My Man

chorus

Now, she was a gal I could count on,
He was my favorite man.
My back was turned for a minute
Right then your fun began.

Verse

I've waited a lifetime for my kind of man
He fills every hope, every dream, every plan.
So you'd better stop it before it's too late
Quit messin' around with my man!

Now he was contented till you showed your face,
A rose in your hair, black satin and lace.
So you'd better listen and take my advice,
Quit messin' around with my man!

You tried so hard with your charms to intrigue him,
Can't blame you, he's so debonair;
But don't you see, all his love and his kisses
I am not willing to share!

So take those swaying hips and that dangerous gown
To some other guy in a faraway town
Cause I'm not the kind to forget and forgive
Quit messin' around with my private plan of a man!

For The Love Of Mike!

Lyrics by Gladys Oakley
Music by Grace Ruff

Chorus:

I was so care-free, light-hearted and gay
Before you happened to pass my way.
Now I'm alone and I'm terribly blue
For there's no one for me, but you!

Verse:

Why do I keep trying to stop in my crying
When my poor heart feels like dying?
It's all I live for, oh, what I'd give for
Just the love of Mike!

Why am I not dating? Why am I kept waiting?
When the spring just calls for mating?
The birds are cooing, but I'm boo-hooing
For the love of Mike.

It's not that he's different,
It's just that he's nice.
I knew that I loved him
When I saw him twice;
But Fate pulled a fast one
And used loaded dice so here I am

Pretending I'm sleeping as I lie here weeping
And my lonely vigil keeping
I can't help moping as I keep hoping
For the love of Mike.

Who Stole Dat Leg?

A novelty song

Chorus:

Now Rastus and his friend, the other night,
Stole a neighbor's chicken in the waning light.
They cooked it up brown and divided it straight;
But the leg that was for Rastus was not upon the plate!

Verse:

Ah's takin out my razor and ah's countin' to ten-
That leg had better be on my platter again.
Now my razor's long and my rezor's sharp.
Say, boy, how's you at playin' the harp?
Who stole dat leg, boy?
Who stole dat leg?

Now they's only you and they's only me,
They ain't nobody else around that ah can see.
So if that leg just took a little walk,
It better hike right back befo' my razor talks.
Who stole dat leg, boy?
Who stole dat leg?

Now you and me, we always been good friends
But this is where our friendship ends
Unless that leg gets back upon my plate
You gonna be a knockin' at the Pearly Gate!
Listen son, you better tell me now
Cause I's gonna find out any how,
Who stole dat leg, boy?
Who stole dat leg?

Tears Run in My Ears

Music by Grace Ruff
Lyrics by Gladys Oakley

Chorus:

They taught me in school, to read and to write,
To add two and two and tell wrong from right;
But they didn't even mention of
That mysterious, delirious subject called 'Love'.

Verse:

I've learned my lesson. I'm wise to the rule
They somehow forgot to teach me in school:
That when a heart is sick with fright,
Tears run in your ears at night!

They taught us to tell true gold from the fake
But they didn't say Love was a pain or an ache
Or that my heart would soar like a kite
Then tears run in my ears at night.

I didn't know you were just having fun,
A sort of a hug and a kiss on the run.
It's over. It's finished. The party is through.

I found love is a game that two must play
And it doesn't do any good to say
"Stay out of my mind for you're out of sight"
Because tears still run in my ears at night!

Michigan National Guard Anthem

Music by Helen Carey
Lyrics by Gladys Oakley
Arrangement by Grace Ruff

Verse 1:

They came from every rock and rill,
Came from each wooded hill
And from the farms.
They left their boats beside the shore,
Some to return no more,
To shoulder arms! To arms!

Chorus:

Oh, raise your voices high to the heroes
Who fought on every land and sea
Each time they heard the battle call to duty
To keep our country gloriously free!
Oh, let their banner proudly unfurl
And shout their name in every tongue
For every time that free men get together
The glory of their battles shall be sung
Forever more! For ever more!

Verse 2:

They came from every walk of life!
Each man to join the strife
For victory,
The trapper came down from his lines,
The miner from his mines
To fight for you and me!

Verse 3:

They manned their guns and planes and tanks,
Each man a fighting Yank,
And crossed the sea.
Wherever hate and fear were found
There did their bugle sound
For Liberty, Liberty!

I Tell My Heart

Lyrics by Gladys Oakley
Music by Grace Ruff

Verse:

I thought I knew my way around,
That I would be so safe and sound,
How could I know that you abound
    With sorrow?
I can see you are not my kind,
Why don't I listen to my mind
It tells me I'll be left behind
    Tomorrow!

Chorus:

I tell my heart it shouldn't sing
Because your words don't mean a thing.
I tell my heart it shouldn't race
Whene'er I chance to see your face.
I tell my heart that with the dawn
I will be here; but you'll be gone.
Each night I lie awake and cry
And sigh, "Oh, fool was I to fall in love".
I'll tell my heart again!

An Unfinished Poem

Oh give me a hat, the ten-gallon kind,
And spurs that sparkle and gleam.
I'll say good-bye to all the towns I have known –
I'll just be a buckaroo.
I'll roam the range where man is free –
Free to yodel or dream.
Gonna meet that girl in a gingham gown;
And kiss her a time or two

I'll buy me a range where the setting sun
Caps all the mountains with gold.
And I'll marry the gal in the gingham gown
And raise me a buckaroo
With three-cornered pants, a ten-gallon hat,
And spurs that sparkle like gold. (Rolled, told)
                      Town, down
                      Oo

    This is a handwritten beginning of a poem that I found. Try your hand at finishing it. If you have an ending for the poem, or even an additional verse, or a title; I would be very interested in hearing from you. This seemed like the perfect poem to end the book. There is enough of the poem to indicate the rhyming. I even included my mom's hints to herself of possible rhymes. I have included this poem exactly as I found it except that I included a title of "Unfinished" to include it in the table of contents.

    Thank you, again, for reading and feel free to contact me, especially with any endings or titles for this poem. You can write me at gailpmain@yahoo.com. Please use the subject Unfinished poem, so I will be able to identify it immediately.

Made in the USA